아서,
도서관에 갇히다!

CONTENTS

대한민국 영어 학습자라면 꼭 한번 읽어봐야 할, 아서 챕터북 시리즈!

아서 챕터북 시리즈(Arthur Chapter Book series)는 미국의 작가 마크 브라운(Marc Brown)이 쓴 책입니다. 레이크우드 초등학교에 다니는 주인공 아서(Arthur)가 소소한 일상에서 벌이는 다양한 에피소드를 담은 이 책은, 기본적으로 미국 초등학생들을 위해 쓰인 책이지만 누구나 공감할 만한 재미있는 스토리로 출간된 지 30년이 넘는 지금까지 남녀노소 모두에게 큰 사랑을 받고 있습니다. 아서가 주인공으로 등장하는 이야기는 리더스북과 챕터북 등 다양한 형태로 출판되었는데, 현재 미국에서만 누적 판매 부수가 6천6백만 부를 돌파한 상황으로 대한민국 인구 숫자보다 더 많은 책이 판매된 것을 생각하면 그 인기가 어느 정도 인지 실감할 수 있습니다.

특히 이 『아서 챕터북』은 한국에서 영어 학습자를 위한 최적의 원서로 큰 사랑을 받고 있기도 합니다. 『영어 낭독 훈련』, 『잠수네 영어 학습법』, 『솔빛이네 엄마표 영어연수』 등 많은 영어 학습법 책들에서 『아서 챕터북』을 추천 도서로 선정하고 있으며, 수많은 영어 고수들과 영어 선생님들, '엄마표 영어'를 진행하는 부모님들에게도 반드시 거쳐 가야 하는 영어원서로 전폭적인 지지를 얻고 있습니다.

번역과 단어장이 포함된 워크북, 그리고 오디오북까지 담긴 풀 패키지!

이 책은 이렇게 큰 사랑을 받고 있는 영어원서 『아서 챕터북』 시리즈에, 더욱 탁월한 학습 효과를 거둘 수 있도록 다양한 콘텐츠를 덧붙인 책입니다.

- 영어원서: 본문에 나온 어려운 어휘에 볼드 처리가 되어 있어 단어를 더욱 분명히 인지하며 자연스럽게 암기하게 됩니다.
- 단어장: 원서에 나온 어려운 어휘가 '한영'은 물론 '영영' 의미까지 완벽하게 정리되어 있으며, 반복되는 단어까지 넣어두어 자연스럽게 복습이 되도록 구성했습니다.
- 번역: 영어와 비교할 수 있도록 직역에 가까운 번역을 담았습니다. 원서 읽기에 익숙하지 않은 초보 학습자들도 어려움 없이 내용을 파악할 수 있습니다.
- 퀴즈: 현직 원어민 교사가 만든 이해력 점검 퀴즈가 들어있습니다.
- 오디오북: 미국 현지에서 판매중인 빠른 속도의 오디오북(분당 약 145단어)과

국내에서 녹음된 따라 읽기용 오디오북(분당 약 110단어)을 포함하고 있어 듣기 훈련은 물론 소리 내어 읽기에까지 폭넓게 사용할 수 있습니다.

이 책의 수준과 타깃 독자

- 미국 원어민 기준: 유치원 ~ 초등학교 저학년
- 한국 학습자 기준: 초등학교 저학년 ~ 중학교 1학년
- 영어원서 완독 경험이 없는 초보 영어 학습자 (토익 기준 450~750점대)
- 비슷한 수준의 다른 챕터북: Magic Tree House, Marvin Redpost, Zack Files, Captain Underpants
- 도서 분량: 5,000단어 초반 (약 5,000~5,200단어)

아서 챕터북, 이렇게 읽어보세요!

- **단어 암기는 이렇게!** 처음 리딩을 시작하기 전, 해당 챕터에 나오는 단어들을 눈으로 쭉 훑어봅니다. 모르는 단어는 좀 더 주의 깊게 보되, 손으로 써가면서 완벽하게 암기할 필요는 없습니다. 본문을 읽으면서 이 단어들을 다시 만나게 되는데, 그 과정에서 단어의 쓰임새와 어감을 자연스럽게 익히게 됩니다. 이렇게 책을 읽은 후에, 단어를 다시 한번 복습하세요. 복습할 때는 중요하다고 생각하는 단어들을 손으로 써가면서 꼼꼼하게 외우는 것도 좋습니다. 이런 방식으로 책을 읽다보면, 많은 단어를 빠르고 부담 없이 익히게 됩니다.

- **리딩할 때는 리딩에만 집중하자!** 원서를 읽는 중간 중간 모르는 단어가 나온다고 워크북을 들춰보거나, 곧바로 번역을 찾아보는 것은 매우 좋지 않은 습관입니다. 모르는 단어나 이해가 가지 않는 문장이 나온다고 해도 펜으로 가볍게 표시만 해두고, 전체적인 맥락을 잡아가며 빠르게 읽어나가세요. 리딩을 할 때는 속도에 대한 긴장감을 잃지 않으면서 리딩에만 집중하는 것이 좋습니다. 모르는 단어와 문장은, 리딩이 끝난 후에 한꺼번에 정리해보는 '리뷰'시간을 갖습니다. 리뷰를 할 때는 번역은 물론 단어장과 사전도 꼼꼼하게 확인하면서 왜 이해가 되지 않았는지 확인해 봅니다.

- **번역 활용은 이렇게!** 이해가 가지 않는 문장은 번역을 통해서 그 의미를 파악할

수 있습니다. 하지만 한국어와 영어는 정확히 1:1 대응이 되지 않기 때문에 번역을 활용하는 데에도 지혜가 필요합니다. 의역이 된 부분까지 억지로 의미를 대응해서 암기하려고 하기보다, 어떻게 그런 의미가 만들어진 것인지 추측하면서 번역은 참고자료로 활용하는 것이 좋습니다.

- **듣기 훈련은 이렇게!** 리스닝 실력을 향상시키길 원한다면 오디오북을 적극적으로 활용하세요. 처음에는 오디오북을 틀어놓고 눈으로 해당 내용을 따라 읽으면서 훈련을 하고, 이것이 익숙해지면 오디오북만 틀어놓고 '귀를 통해' 책을 읽어보세요. 눈으로는 한 번도 읽지 않은 책을 귀를 통해 완벽하게 이해할 수 있다면 이후에는 영어 듣기로 고생하는 일은 거의 없을 것입니다.

- **소리 내어 읽고 녹음하자!** 이 책은 특히 소리 내어 읽기(Voice Reading)에 최적화된 문장 길이와 구조를 가지고 있습니다. 또한 오디오북 CD에 포함된 '따라 읽기용' 오디오북으로 소리 내어 읽기 훈련을 함께할 수 있습니다. 소리 내어 읽기를 하면서 내가 읽은 것을 녹음하고 들어보세요! 자신의 영어 발음을 들어보는 것은 몹시 민망한 일이지만, 그 과정을 통해서 의식적·무의식적으로 발음을 교정하게 됩니다. 이렇게 영어로 소리를 만들어 본 경험은 이후 탄탄한 스피킹 실력의 밑거름이 될 것입니다.

- **2~3번 반복해서 읽자!** 영어 초보자라면 2~3회 반복해서 읽을 것을 추천합니다. 초보자일수록 처음 읽을 때는 생소한 단어들과 스토리 때문에 내용 파악에 급급할 수밖에 없습니다. 하지만 일단 내용을 파악한 후에 다시 읽으면 어휘와 문장 구조 등 다른 부분까지 관찰하면서 조금 더 깊이 있게 읽을 수 있고, 그 과정에서 리딩 속도도 빨라지고 리딩 실력을 더 확고하게 다지게 됩니다.

- **'시리즈'로 꾸준히 읽자!** 한 작가의 책을 시리즈로 읽는 것 또한 영어 실력 향상에 큰 도움이 됩니다. 같은 등장인물이 다시 나오기 때문에 내용 파악이 더 수월할 뿐 아니라, 작가가 사용하는 어휘와 표현들도 자연스럽게 반복되기 때문에 탁월한 복습 효과까지 얻을 수 있습니다. 『아서 챕터북』 시리즈는 현재 10권, 총 50,000단어 분량이 출간되어 있습니다. 이 책들을 시리즈로 꾸준히 읽으면서 영어 실력을 쑥쑥 향상시켜 보세요!

영어원서 본문 구성

내용이 담긴 본문입니다.
원어민이 읽는 일반 원서와 같은 텍스트지만, 암기해야 할 중요 어휘들은 볼드체로 표시되어 있습니다. 이 어휘들은 지금 들고 계신 워크북에 챕터별로 정리되어 있습니다.

학습 심리학 연구 결과에 따르면, 한 단어씩 따로 외우는 단어 암기는 거의 효과가 없다고 합니다. 대신 단어를 제대로 외우기 위해서는 문맥(Context) 속에서 단어를 암기해야 하며, 한 단어 당 문맥 속에서 15번 이상 마주칠 때 완벽하게 암기할 수 있다고 합니다.

이 책의 본문은 중요 어휘를 볼드로 강조하여, 문맥 속의 단어들을 더 확실히 인지(Word Cognition in Context)하도록 돕고 있습니다. 또한 대부분의 중요한 단어들은 다른 챕터에서도 반복해서 등장하기 때문에 이 책을 읽는 것만으로도 자연스럽게 어휘력을 향상시킬 수 있습니다.

또한 본문에는 내용 이해를 돕기 위해 '각주'가 첨가되어 있습니다. 각주는 굳이 암기할 필요는 없지만, 알아두면 내용을 더 깊이 있게 이해할 수 있어 원서를 읽는 재미가 배가됩니다.

워크북(Workbook)의 구성

Check Your Reading Speed
해당 챕터의 단어 수가 기록되어 있어, 리딩 속도를 측정할 수 있습니다. 특히 리딩 속도를 중시하는 독자들이 유용하게 사용할 수 있습니다.

Build Your Vocabulary
본문에 볼드 표시되어 있는 단어들이 정리되어 있습니다. 리딩 전, 후에 반복해서 보면 원서를 더욱 쉽게 읽을 수 있고, 어휘력도 빠르게 향상됩니다.

단어는 〈빈도 – 스펠링 – 발음기호 – 품사 – 한글 뜻 – 영문 뜻〉 순서로 표기되어 있으며 빈도 표시(★)가 많을수록 필수 어휘입니다. 반복 등장하는 단어는 빈도 대신 '복습'으로 표기되어 있습니다. 품사는 아래와 같이 표기했습니다.

n. 명사 | a. 형용사 | ad. 부사 | v. 동사
conj. 접속사 | prep. 전치사 | int. 감탄사 | idiom 숙어 및 관용구

Comprehension Quiz
간단한 퀴즈를 통해 읽은 내용에 대한 이해력을 점검해 볼 수 있습니다.

번역
영문과 비교할 수 있도록 최대한 직역에 가까운 번역을 담았습니다.

오디오북 CD 구성

이 책은 '듣기 훈련'과 '소리 내어 읽기 훈련'을
위한 2가지 종류의 오디오북이 포함되어 있습
니다.
- 듣기 훈련용 오디오북: 분당 145단어 속도
  (미국 현지 판매 중인 오디오북)
- 소리 내어 읽기 훈련용 오디오북: 분당 110
  단어 속도

오디오북은 MP3 파일로 제공되는 MP3 기기나
컴퓨터에 옮겨서 사용하셔야 합니다. 오디오북
에 이상이 있을 경우 helper@longtailbooks.co.kr로 메일을 주시면 자세한 안내를
받으실 수 있습니다.

EBS 동영상 강의 안내

EBS의 어학사이트(EBSlang.co.kr)에서 『아서 챕터북』 동영상 강의가 진행되고 있습니다.
영어 어순의 원리에 맞게 빠르고 정확하게 이해하는 법을 완벽하게 코치해주는 국내 유일의 강의!
저렴한 수강료에 완강 시 50% 환급까지!
지금 바로 열광적인 수강 평가와 샘플 강의를 확인하세요!

http://www.EBSreading.com

Chapter 1

1. Why was Francine upset with Arthur?

A. Arthur had eaten Francine's lunch.

B. Arthur had said that Francine was mean.

C. Arthur had stopped spending time with Francine.

D. Arthur had said that Francine looked like a marshmallow.

2. Why did Arthur do what he had done?

A. Arthur forgot his own lunch at home.

B. Francine had worn a goofy sweater.

C. Arthur liked hanging out with Buster.

D. Buster told him to do it.

3. Why did Arthur say that the problem was Buster's fault?

A. Buster had talked tough to Francine.

B. Buster liked picking fights with other kids.

C. Buster was jealous of Francine liking Arthur.

D. Buster had made Arhur say mean things about Francine.

4. What did Buster think of the note that was sent to Arthur?

A. He thought that Arthur should send a reply.

B. He thought that the problem was solved.

C. He thought that it was a bad sign.

D. He thought that it was silly.

5. What kind of project were Arthur and Francine assigned to do as a team?

A. An oral report on a hero or heroine

B. A short story about a heroic adventure

C. A report on a trip to the school library

D. A presentation on bullying in their school

$$\frac{529 \ words}{reading \ time \ (\quad) \ sec} \times 60 = (\quad) \ WPM$$

Build Your Vocabulary

belong [bilɔ́:ŋ] v. ~에 속하다; 제자리에 있다: 소속감을 느끼다
You say that something belongs to a particular person when you are guessing, discovering, or explaining that it was produced by or is part of that person.

charge [ʧɑːrdʒ] v. 급히 가다, 달려가다; 청구하다; 기소하다; n. 요금; 책임, 담당
If you charge toward someone or something, you move quickly and aggressively toward them.

fold [fould] v. (두 손·팔 등을) 끼다; 접다; 감싸다; n. 주름; 접는 부분
If you fold your arms or hands, you bring them together and cross or link them, for example over your chest.

nod [nad] v. (고개를) 끄덕이다, 끄덕여 나타내다; n. (고개를) 끄덕임
If you nod, you move your head downward and upward to show agreement, understanding, or approval.

goofy [gúːfi] a. 바보 같은, 얼빠진
If you describe someone or something as goofy, you think they are rather silly or ridiculous.

puff up idiom 부풀어오르다, 불룩해지다
If something puffs up, or if you puff it up, it looks bigger, usually because it has air in it.

pad [pæd] v. ~에 속을 넣다; 소리 안 나게 걷다; n. 패드; 보호대
(padded a. 속을 채워 넣은)
If you pad something, you put something soft in it or over it in order to make it less hard, to protect it, or to give it a different shape.

fluff [flʌf] v. 부풀리다; n. 보풀, 솜털
If you fluff out something like cushions or feathers, you make them appear fuller and softer by shaking or brushing them.

ignore [ignɔ́ːr] v. 무시하다; (사람을) 못 본 척하다
If you ignore someone or something, you pay no attention to them.

stare [stɛər] v. 빤히 쳐다보다, 응시하다; n. 빤히 쳐다보기, 응시
If you stare at someone or something, you look at them for a long time.

or else idiom (협박·경고의 의미로) 안 그랬단 봐; 그렇지 않으면
You say 'or else' after a command to warn someone that if they do not obey, you will be angry and may harm or punish them.

get it idiom 혼이 나다, 야단맞다, 벌받다; 이해하다
If you say someone is going to get it, you mean they will be punished or spoken to angrily about something.

toss [tɔːs] v. (고개를) 홱 쳐들다; 던지다; n. 던지기
If you toss your head or toss your hair, you move your head backward, quickly and suddenly, often expressing an emotion such as anger.

sigh [sai] v. 한숨을 쉬다, 한숨짓다; n. 한숨; 탄식
When you sigh, you let out a deep breath, as a way of expressing feelings such as disappointment, tiredness, or pleasure.

glare [glɛər] v. 노려보다; 눈부시다; n. 노려봄; 눈부심
If you glare at someone, you look at them with an angry expression on your face.

fault [fɔːlt] n. 잘못, 책임; 단점; 결함; v. 나무라다, 흠잡다
If a bad or undesirable situation is your fault, you caused it or are responsible for it.

wedge [wedʒ] v. 밀어 넣다; 고정시키다; n. 쐐기
If you wedge something somewhere, you fit it there tightly.

tough [tʌf] a. 억센, 거친; 힘든, 어려운; 엄한, 냉정한
If you describe someone as tough, you mean that they are rough and violent.

stand up for idiom ~을 옹호하다
If you stand up for someone or something, you support or defend them, especially when someone else is criticizing them.

land [lænd] v. 떨어지다; 내려앉다, 착륙하다; n. 육지; 땅, 지역
When someone or something lands, they come down to the ground after moving through the air or falling.

warning [wɔ́:rniŋ] n. 경고, 주의
A warning is something which is said or written to tell people of a possible danger, problem, or other unpleasant thing that might happen.

grab [græb] v. 붙잡다, 움켜잡다; n. 와락 잡아채려고 함
If you grab something, you take it or pick it up suddenly and roughly.

pause [pɔːz] v. (말·일을 하다가) 잠시 멈추다; 정지시키다; n. 멈춤
If you pause while you are doing something, you stop for a short period and then continue.

sign [sain] n. 징후, 흔적; 몸짓; v. 서명하다; 신호를 보내다
If there is a sign of something, there is something which shows that it exists or is happening.

attention [əténʃən] n. 주의, 주목; 관심
If you give someone or something your attention, you look at it, listen to it, or think about it carefully.

consider [kənsídər] v. 고려하다, 숙고하다; 여기다
If you are considering doing something, you intend to do it, but have not yet made a final decision whether to do it.

zip [zip] v. (어떤 방향으로) 쌩 하고 가다; 지퍼로 잠그다; n. 지퍼
If something or someone zips somewhere, they move there very quickly.

blackboard [blǽkbɔ̀:rd] n. 칠판
A blackboard is a dark-colored board that you can write on with chalk.

wonder [wʌ́ndər] v. 궁금해하다; (크게) 놀라다; n. 경탄, 경이
If you wonder about something, you think about it because it interests you and you want to know more about it.

generous [dʒénərəs] a. 관대한, 아량 있는; 너그러운
A generous person is friendly, helpful, and willing to see the good qualities in someone or something.

puzzle [pʌzl] v. 어리둥절하게 하다; n. 퍼즐; 수수께끼 (puzzled a. 당혹스러운)
Someone who is puzzled is confused because they do not understand something.

be supposed to idiom ~하기로 되어 있다; ~해야 한다
If you are supposed to do something, you are required to do it because of the position you are in or an agreement you have made.

go on idiom 말을 계속하다; (어떤 상황이) 계속되다; 시작하다
When you go on, you continue speaking after a short pause.

groan [groun] v. 신음 소리를 내다, 끙끙거리다; n. 신음, 끙 하는 소리
If you groan, you make a long, low sound because you are in pain, or because you are upset or unhappy about something.

prepare [pripéər] v. 준비하다; 대비하다, 각오하다
If you prepare something, you make it ready for something that is going to happen.

oral [ɔ́:rəl] a. 구두(口頭)의, 구술의
Oral communication is spoken rather than written.

pair [pɛər] n. 짝, 두 사람; 한 쌍; v. (둘씩) 짝을 짓다
You can refer to two people as a pair when they are standing or walking together or when they have some kind of relationship with each other.

consult [kənsʌ́lt] v. 찾아보다, 참고하다; 상담하다

If you consult a book or a map, you look in it or look at it in order to find some information.

glance [glæns] v. 흘낏 보다; 대충 훑어보다; n. 흘낏 봄

If you glance at something or someone, you look at them very quickly and then look away again immediately.

Chapter 2

1. **Which was NOT one of the heroes that Arthur and Buster mentioned while walking home?**
   A. Superman
   B. Robin Hood
   C. Hercules
   D. The Bionic Bunny

2. **Who was D.W. talking to on the phone?**
   A. Buster
   B. Francine
   C. Her mother
   D. Arthur

3. What did D.W. say that Arthur looked like in his pajamas?

A. She said that he looked like a pirate.

B. She said that he looked like a marshmallow.

C. She said that he looked like a soggy dumpling.

D. She said that he looked like a fat baby.

4. Why did D.W. have to give Arthur a message?

A. Arthur had lost his phone.

B. Arthur had returned home late.

C. Francine was not speaking to Arthur.

D. Arthur was not allowed to use the phone.

5. What did the message say?

A. Francine would do the whole school project by herself.

B. Francine would meet him at the library tomorrow at three.

C. Francine had chosen a different partner for the school project.

D. Francine wanted Arthur to go buy some movies about heroes.

Check Your Reading Speed
1분에 몇 단어를 읽는지 리딩 속도를 측정해보세요.

$$\frac{473 \text{ words}}{\text{reading time (} \quad \text{) sec}} \times 60 = (\quad) \text{ WPM}$$

Build Your Vocabulary

⚝ **favorite** [féivərit] n. 마음에 드는 사람, 좋아하는 물건; a. 마음에 드는, 매우 좋아하는
A favorite is a person or thing that is preferred to all others of the same kind or is especially well liked.

복습 **nod** [nad] v. (고개를) 끄덕이다, 끄덕여 나타내다; n. (고개를) 끄덕임
If you nod, you move your head downward and upward to show agreement, understanding, or approval.

⚝ **exact** [igzǽkt] a. 정확한, 정밀한; 엄격한 (exactly ad. 맞아; 정확히, 틀림없이)
If you say 'Exactly,' you are agreeing with someone or emphasizing the truth of what they say.

⚝ **heroic** [hiróuik] a. 용감무쌍한, 영웅적인; 투지 넘치는
If you describe a person or their actions as heroic, you admire them because they show extreme bravery.

복습 **pause** [pɔ:z] v. (말·일을 하다가) 잠시 멈추다; 정지시키다; n. 멈춤
If you pause while you are doing something, you stop for a short period and then continue.

⚝ **certain** [sə:rtn] a. 확실한, 틀림없는; 확신하는 (certainly ad. 분명히)
You use certainly to emphasize what you are saying when you are making a statement.

⚝ **gasp** [gæsp] v. 숨이 턱 막히다, 헉 하고 숨을 쉬다; n. 헉 하는 소리를 냄
When you gasp, you take a short quick breath through your mouth, especially when you are surprised, shocked, or in pain.

go on idiom 말을 계속하다; (어떤 상황이) 계속되다; 시작하다
When you go on, you continue speaking after a short pause.

suppose [səpóuz] v. (~이라고) 생각하다, 추측하다; 가정하다
If you suppose that something is true, you believe that it is probably true, because of other things that you know.

glare [glɛər] v. 노려보다; 눈부시다; n. 노려봄; 눈부심
If you glare at someone, you look at them with an angry expression on your face.

lately [léitli] ad. 최근에, 얼마 전에
You use lately to describe events in the recent past, or situations that started a short time ago.

ignore [ignɔ́:r] v. 무시하다; (사람을) 못 본 척하다
If you ignore someone or something, you pay no attention to them.

pajamas [pədʒáːməz] n. (바지와 상의로 된) 잠옷
A pair of pajamas consists of loose trousers and a loose jacket that people wear in bed.

give up idiom 포기하다; 그만두다; 단념하다
If you give something up, you stop trying to do it or having it.

soggy [sági] a. 질척한, 질척거리는
Something that is soggy is unpleasantly wet.

reach [riːʧ] v. (손·팔을) 뻗다, 내밀다; 이르다, 도달하다; n. 거리; 범위
If you reach somewhere, you move your arm and hand to take or touch something.

hang up idiom 전화를 끊다, 수화기를 놓다
If you hang up the phone, you end a telephone conversation, often very suddenly.

go around idiom (자주) ~하다, ~하고 다니다
If you go around doing something, you spend your time behaving badly or doing something that is unpleasant for other people.

expect [ikspékt] v. 예상하다, 기대하다; 요구하다
If you expect something, or expect a person to do something, you believe that it is your right to have that thing, or the person's duty to do it for you.

big deal [bíg díːl] n. 대단한 것, 큰 일; int. 그게 무슨 대수라고!
If you say that something is a big deal, you mean that it is important or significant in some way.

impress [imprés] v. 깊은 인상을 주다, 감명을 주다; 새기다 (impressed a. 감명을 받은)
If something impresses you, you feel great admiration for it.

roll one's eyes idiom 눈을 굴리다
If you roll your eyes, you move them round and upward when you are frightened, bored, or annoyed.

sigh [sai] v. 한숨을 쉬다, 한숨짓다; n. 한숨; 탄식
When you sigh, you let out a deep breath, as a way of expressing feelings such as disappointment, tiredness, or pleasure.

stick one's nose in the air idiom 오만하게 굴다, 거들먹거리다
If someone sticks their nose in the air, they behave in a way that shows that they think they are better than other people.

blame [bleim] v. ~을 탓하다, ~의 책임으로 보다; n. 책임; 탓
If you blame a person or thing for something bad, you believe or say that they are responsible for it or that they caused it.

be supposed to idiom ~하기로 되어 있다; ~해야 한다
If you are supposed to do something, you are required to do it because of the position you are in or an agreement you have made.

wag [wæg] v. (손가락·고개를) 흔들다; n. 흔들기
If you wag your finger, you shake it repeatedly and quickly from side to side, usually because you are annoyed with someone.

call names idiom ~를 나쁘게 말하다, 흉보다
If someone calls you names, they insult you by saying unpleasant things to you or about you.

* **mess** [mes] n. 엉망인 상황; (지저분하고) 엉망인 상태; v. 엉망으로 만들다

If you say that a situation is a mess, you mean that it is full of trouble or problems. You can also say that something is in a mess.

Chapter 3

1. How did Arthur lose track of the time before going to the library?

A. He was watching his favorite TV show.

B. He was playing outside with Pal.

C. He was eating breakfast with his parents.

D. He was thinking of a way to apologize to Francine.

2. Why did Arthur not want to be late to the library?

A. He wanted to get the best books before they were checked out.

B. He wanted to meet Buster before he had to meet Francine.

C. He thought Francine would complain about him being late.

D. He wanted to find a good spot to study with Francine.

3. Who did Ms. Turner suggest as a hero?

A. Joan of Arc

B. Jane Goodall

C. George Washington

D. Genghis Khan

4. Why did Francine get to check the biographies?

A. She knew where to find them.

B. She was at the library first.

C. She knew very little about history.

D. She wanted to stay away from Arthur.

5. What did Ms. Turner tell Arthur and Francine not to forget?

A. To check out the books

B. To return the books

C. The fact that the help desk was open

D. The fact that the library closed at five

Check Your Reading Speed
1분에 몇 단어를 읽는지 리딩 속도를 측정해보세요.

$$\frac{482 \text{ words}}{\text{reading time ( ) sec}} \times 60 = (\qquad) \text{ WPM}$$

Build Your Vocabulary

strike [straik] v. (struck–stricken/struck) (시계가) 치다; 부딪치다; n. 파업; 공격
When a clock strikes, its bells make a sound to indicate what the time is.

backyard [bǽkjá:rd] n. 뒷마당, 뒤뜰
A backyard is an area of land at the back of a house.

lose track of idiom ~을 놓치다, 잊다
If you lose track of someone or something, you no longer know where they are or what is happening.

complain [kəmpléin] v. 불평하다, 투덜거리다
If you complain about a situation, you say that you are not satisfied with it.

librarian [laibréəriən] n. (도서관의) 사서
A librarian is a person who is in charge of a library or who has been specially trained to work in a library.

reference [réfərəns] n. 문의, 조회; 참고; 언급 (reference desk n. 안내데스크)
Reference is the act of consulting someone or something in order to get information or advice.

consult [kənsʌ́lt] v. 찾아보다, 참고하다; 상담하다
If you consult a book or a map, you look in it or look at it in order to find some information.

26

use up idiom ~을 다 쓰다; 다 써버리다
If you use up something, you use all of them until no more is left.

glare [glɛər] n. 노려봄; 눈부심; v. 노려보다; 눈부시다
A glare is an angry, hard, and unfriendly look.

work on idiom (해결하기 위해) ~에 애쓰다; (원하는) 효과가 나다
If you work on something such as a particular activity, project, or piece of research, you are busy with it.

charge [ʧɑːrdʒ] n. 책임, 담당; 요금; v. 급히 가다, 달려가다; 청구하다; 기소하다
If you take charge of someone or something, you make yourself responsible for them and take control over them.

fold [fould] v. (두 손·팔 등을) 끼다; 접다; 감싸다; n. 주름; 접는 부분
If you fold your arms or hands, you bring them together and cross or link them, for example over your chest.

think up idiom ~을 생각해 내다, 고안하다
If you think something up, you create an idea, a plan, or a story in your mind.

insult [insʌ́lt] n. 모욕(적인 말·행동); v. 모욕하다
An insult is a rude remark, or something a person says or does which insults you.

discuss [diskʌ́s] v. 의논하다, 논의하다; 논하다
If people discuss something, they talk about it, often in order to reach a decision.

further [fɔ́ːrðər] ad. 더; 더 멀리에; a. 더 이상의, 추가의; v. 발전시키다
If someone goes further in a discussion, they make a more extreme statement or deal with a point more thoroughly.

inspirational [inspəréiʃənl] a. 영감을 주는, 자극을 주는
Something that is inspirational provides you with a feeling of enthusiasm.

put in idiom (남이 말하는데) 끼어들다; (편지·이야기 등에) ~을 집어넣다
When you put in, you intervene with a remark during a conversation.

sort [sɔːrt] n. 종류, 유형; v. 분류하다, 구분하다
You describe someone as a particular sort when you are describing their character.

get under control idiom ~을 제어하게 되다
If you get something under control, you deal with it successfully and it is unlikely to cause any more harm.

heroic [hiróuik] a. 용감무쌍한, 영웅적인; 투지 넘치는
If you describe a person or their actions as heroic, you admire them because they show extreme bravery.

turn red idiom (얼굴 등이) 빨개지다
When you turn red, you get red in the face because you are embarrassed.

think out loud idiom 생각나는 대로 말하다
If you think out loud, you express your thoughts as they occur to you, rather than thinking first and then speaking.

tap [tæp] v. (가볍게) 톡톡 두드리다; n. (가볍게) 두드리기; 수도꼭지
If you tap something, you hit it with a quick light blow or a series of quick light blows.

counter [káuntər] n. (은행·상점 등의) 계산대, 판매대; v. 반박하다; a. 반대의
In a place such as a shop or café a counter is a long narrow table or flat surface at which customers are served.

certain [sə́ːrtn] a. 확실한, 틀림없는; 확신하는 (certainly ad. 분명히)
You use certainly to emphasize what you are saying when you are making a statement.

lead [liːd] ① v. 지휘하다; 선두를 달리다; 이끌다; n. 선두, 우세 (leader n. 지휘관; 지도자) ② n. [광물] 납
The leader of a group of people or an organization is the person who is in control of it or in charge of it.

history [hístəri] n. 역사; 역사(학)
You can refer to the events of the past as history. You can also refer to the past events which concern a particular topic or place as its history.

inspiration [inspəréiʃən] n. 영감; 영감을 주는 것
Inspiration is a feeling of enthusiasm you get from someone or something, which gives you new and creative ideas.

army [á:rmi] n. 군대; 육군; 부대, 집단
An army is a large organized group of people who are armed and trained to fight on land in a war.

battle [bætl] n. 전투; 투쟁; 싸움; v. 싸우다, 투쟁하다
A battle is a violent fight between groups of people, especially one between military forces during a war.

invade [invéid] v. 침입하다, 침략하다; 난입하다; 침해하다 (invader n. 침략자)
To invade a country means to enter it by force with an army.

stuff [stʌf] n. 것(들), 물건; v. 채워 넣다; 쑤셔 넣다
You can use stuff to refer to things such as a substance, a collection of things, events, or ideas, or the contents of something in a general way without mentioning the thing itself by name.

section [sékʃən] n. 부분, 구획; 부서; v. 구획하다, 구분하다
A section of something is one of the parts into which it is divided or from which it is formed.

biography [baiágrəfi] n. 전기
A biography of someone is an account of their life, written by someone else.

stare [stɛər] v. 빤히 쳐다보다, 응시하다; n. 빤히 쳐다보기, 응시
If you stare at someone or something, you look at them for a long time.

goodness [gúdnis] int. (놀람을 나타내어) 와, 어머나!
People sometimes say 'goodness' or 'my goodness' to express surprise.

enthusiasm [inθú:ziæzm] n. 열정, 열의
Enthusiasm is great eagerness to be involved in a particular activity which you like and enjoy or which you think is important.

frown [fraun] v. 얼굴을 찌푸리다; n. 찡그림, 찌푸림
When someone frowns, their eyebrows become drawn together, because they are annoyed or puzzled.

stick out idiom ~을 내밀다, 튀어나오게 하다
If you stick something out, you make something, especially part of your body, come through a hole.

tongue [tʌŋ] n. 혀
Your tongue is the soft movable part inside your mouth which you use for tasting, eating, and speaking.

stack [stæk] n. (pl.) (도서관의) 서가; 무더기, 더미; v. 쌓다, 포개다; 채우다
The stacks refer to storage space in a library consisting of an extensive arrangement of bookshelves where most of the books are stored.

medieval [mìːdíːvəl] a. 중세의
Something that is medieval relates to or was made in the period of European history between 476 AD and about 1500 AD.

head [hed] v. (특정 방향으로) 향하다; ~을 이끌다; n. 머리, 고개; 책임자
If you are heading for a particular place, you are going toward that place.

aisle [ail] n. 통로
An aisle is a long narrow gap that people can walk along between rows of seats in a public building.

prompt [prampt] a. 시간을 엄수하는; 즉각적인, 지체 없는; v. 촉발하다; 유도하다
(promptly ad. 정확히 제 시간에; 지체 없이)
If you do something promptly, at a particular time, you do it at exactly that time.

Chapter 4

1. How did Ms. Turner impress Arthur?

A. She knew how to solve problems between friends.

B. She could read so many interesting books so quickly.

C. She knew where to send him without looking anything up.

D. She knew exactly what kind of books Arthur liked reading.

2. What kind of book did Arthur find?

A. A book on French history

B. A book on English history

C. A book about medieval fantasy

D. A book about unicorns and wizards

3. **Why were the French attacking Arthur in his dream?**

A. Arthur was an English knight who had conquered France.

B. Arthur had called the French general a marshmallow.

C. Arthur had shot an arrow at the French general.

D. Arthur had stopped learning to speak French.

4. **What kind of book did Francine find?**

A. A book about France

B. A book about Joan of Arc

C. A book about English armies

D. A book about armor and swords

5. **Why had Francine brought a Walkman with her?**

A. She wanted to listen to French.

B. She wanted to let Arthur listen to a song.

C. She wanted to listen to music to help her take a nap.

D. She wanted to listen to music to help her ignore Arthur.

$$\frac{488 \ words}{reading \ time \ (\quad) \ sec} \times 60 = (\quad) \ WPM$$

Build Your Vocabulary

history [hístəri] n. 역사; 역사(학)
You can refer to the events of the past as history. You can also refer to the past events which concern a particular topic or place as its history.

impress [imprés] v. 깊은 인상을 주다, 감명을 주다; 새기다 (impressed a. 감명을 받은)
If something impresses you, you feel great admiration for it.

confuse [kənfjúːz] v. (사람을) 혼란시키다; 혼동하다 (confusing a. 혼란스러운)
Something that is confusing makes it difficult for people to know exactly what is happening or what to do.

decorate [dékərèit] v. 장식하다, 꾸미다 (decorated a. 훌륭하게 꾸민, 장식된)
If you decorate something, you make it more attractive by adding things to it.

conquer [káŋkər] v. 정복하다; 이기다; 극복하다
If one country or group of people conquers another, they take complete control of their land.

settle [setl] v. (편하게) 앉다; 해결하다, 끝내다; 결정하다
If you settle yourself somewhere or settle somewhere, you sit down or make yourself comfortable.

comfortable [kʌ́mfərtəbl] a. 편안한, 쾌적한; 편하게 생각하는
If a piece of furniture or an item of clothing is comfortable, it makes you feel physically relaxed when you use it, for example because it is soft.

get through idiom ~을 하다, 끝내다; 써 버리다; ~에게 전달되다
To get through something means to manage to do or complete it.

eyelid [áilid] n. 눈꺼풀
Your eyelids are the two pieces of skin which cover your eyes when they are closed.

slump [slʌmp] v. 털썩 앉다; 급감하다, 급락하다; n. 급감, 폭락; 불황
If you slump somewhere, you fall or sit down there heavily, for example because you are very tired or you feel ill.

look out idiom 주의해라!, 조심해라!
When you say 'look out' to someone, you tell them to be careful, especially when there is some danger.

duck [dʌk] v. (머리나 몸을) 휙 숙이다; 피하다; 급히 움직이다; n. [동물] 오리
If you duck, you move your head or the top half of your body quickly downward to avoid something that might hit you, or to avoid being seen.

arrow [ǽrou] n. 화살; 화살표
An arrow is a long thin weapon which is sharp and pointed at one end and which often has feathers at the other end.

whiz [hwiz] v. 쌩 하고 움직이다; n. 윙 하는 소리
If something whizzes somewhere, it moves there very fast.

harmless [há:rmlis] a. 해가 없는, 무해한; 악의 없는
(harmlessly ad. 해를 끼치지 않게)
Something that is harmless does not have any bad effects, especially on people's health.

aim [eim] n. 겨냥, 조준; 목표; v. 목표하다; 겨누다
Your aim is your skill or action in pointing a weapon or other object at its target.

practice [prǽktis] v. 연습하다; 실행하다; n. 연습, 훈련; 실행
If you practice something, you keep doing it regularly in order to be able to do it better.

perch [pəːrtʃ] n. 높은 위치; v. (무엇의 꼭대기나 끝에) 위치하다
A perch is a place where someone or something rests or sits, especially one that is high or precarious.

battle [bætl] n. 전투; 투쟁; 싸움; v. 싸우다, 투쟁하다
A battle is a violent fight between groups of people, especially one between military forces during a war.

army [áːrmi] n. 군대; 육군; 부대, 집단
An army is a large organized group of people who are armed and trained to fight on land in a war.

gather [gǽðər] v. (사람들이) 모이다; (여기저기 있는 것을) 모으다
If people gather somewhere or if someone gathers people somewhere, they come together in a group.

force [fɔːrs] n. 집단; 무장 병력; 물리력, 폭력; v. 강요하다, 억지로 ~하다
When people do something in force, they do it in large numbers.

moat [mout] n. 호, 해자(성 주위에 둘러 판 못)
A moat is a deep, wide channel dug round a place such as a castle and filled with water, in order to protect the place from attack.

take offense at idiom ~에 대해 화를 내다; ~에 기분이 상하다
If someone takes offense at something you say or do, they feel upset, often unnecessarily, because they think you are being rude to them.

regret [rigrét] v. 후회하다; 유감스럽게 생각하다; n. 유감, 애석; 후회
If you regret something that you have done, you wish that you had not done it.

proud [praud] a. 자존심이 강한; 자랑스러워 하는; 오만한, 거만한
Someone who is proud has respect for themselves and does not want to lose the respect that other people have for them.

admit [ædmít] v. 인정하다, 시인하다
If you admit that something bad, unpleasant, or embarrassing is true, you agree, often unwillingly, that it is true.

mood [muːd] n. 기분; 분위기
Your mood is the way you are feeling at a particular time.

apologize [əpálədʒàiz] v. 사과하다 (apology n. 사과; 변명)
An apology is something that you say or write in order to tell someone that you are sorry that you have hurt them or caused trouble for them.

ride [raid] v. (말·자전거·차량 등을) 타다; n. (차량·자전거 등을) 타고 달리기; 여정
When you ride a horse, you sit on it and control its movements.

back and forth [bæk ən fɔ́ːrθ] idiom 앞뒤로; 좌우로; 여기저기에, 왔다 갔다
If someone moves back and forth, they repeatedly move in one direction and then in the opposite direction.

troop [truːp] n. (대규모의) 병력, 군대; 무리; v. 무리를 지어 걸어가다
Troops are soldiers, especially when they are in a large organized group doing a particular task.

somehow [sámhàu] ad. 왜 그런지 (모르겠지만), 왠지
You use somehow to say that you do not know or cannot say how something was done or will be done.

cheer [ʧiər] v. 환호성을 지르다; 힘을 북돋우다; n. 환호(성)
When people cheer, they shout loudly to show their approval or to encourage someone who is doing something such as taking part in a game.

bong [baŋ] n. 둥, 뎅그렁뎅그렁 (하고 큰 종이 울리는 소리)
A bong is a long, deep sound such as the sound made by a big bell.

private [práivət] a. 혼자 있을 수 있는; 사유의; 사적인; 은밀한
If you describe a place as private, you mean that it is a quiet place and you can be alone there without being disturbed.

stay put idiom (있던 자리에) 그대로 있다
If you stay put, you remain somewhere.

risk [risk] v. ~의 위험을 무릅쓰다; ~을 위태롭게 하다; n. 위험; 위험 요소
If you risk doing something, you do it, even though you know that it might have undesirable consequences.

run into idiom ~를 우연히 만나다, ~와 마주치다
If you run into someone, you meet them by chance.

cross-legged [krɔːs-légtd] ad. 책상다리를 하고
If someone is sitting cross-legged, they are sitting on the floor with their legs bent so that their knees point outward.

easily [íːzili] ad. 수월하게, 용이하게; 쉽게, 잘
You use easily to emphasize that something is very likely to happen, or is very likely to be true.

ignore [ignɔ́ːr] v. 무시하다; (사람을) 못 본 척하다
If you ignore someone or something, you pay no attention to them.

lead [liːd] ① v. (led–led) 지휘하다; 선두를 달리다; 이끌다; n. 선두, 우세 ② n. [광물] 납
If you lead a group of people, an organization, or an activity, you are in control or in charge of the people or the activity.

defeat [difíːt] v. 패배시키다, 물리치다; 이해가 안 되다; n. 패배; 타도
If you defeat someone, you win a victory over them in a battle, game, or contest.

maid [meid] n. 처녀, 아가씨; 하녀, 가정부
A maid is a young unmarried girl or woman.

armor [áːrmər] n. 갑옷, 철갑; 무기; v. ~에게 갑옷을 입히다
Armor is a defensive covering, as of metal, wood, or leather, worn to protect the body against weapons.

sword [sɔːrd] n. 검(劍), 칼
A sword is a weapon with a handle and a long sharp blade.

wonder [wʌ́ndər] v. 궁금해하다; (크게) 놀라다; n. 경탄, 경이
If you wonder about something, you think about it because it interests you and you want to know more about it.

hum [hʌm] v. 콧노래를 부르다, (노래를) 흥얼거리다; n. 웅웅거리는 소리
When you hum a tune, you sing it with your lips closed.

fade [feid] v. 서서히 사라지다; 바래다, 희미해지다
When light fades, it slowly becomes less bright.

aisle [ail] n. 통로
An aisle is a long narrow gap that people can walk along between rows of seats in a public building.

Chapter
5

1. **Which of the following was NOT something that Arthur noticed when he woke up?**

   A. The clock was broken.

   B. The library was quiet.

   C. The front door was locked.

   D. Many of the lights were turned off.

2. **How did Arthur feel about being in a closed library?**

   A. He thought that it was exciting.

   B. He thought that it could be an adventure.

   C. He wished his friends could be there with him.

   D. He was scared and wondered how it could have happened.

3. Why did Arthur think that he might not be alone in the library?

A. He heard someone talking.

B. He heard a crashing sound.

C. He saw the books move around.

D. He thought that Francine might be looking for him.

4. What did Arthur do when he reached the stairwell?

A. He called out for help.

B. He bravely went down the stairs.

C. He grabbed a flashlight and went down.

D. He looked up and down the stairs and listened carefully.

5. What happened just as Arthur was beginning to relax and concentrate on getting out of the library?

A. A hand grabbed his shoulder from behind.

B. Francine called out his name from behind.

C. He heard another crashing sound.

D. The lights in the library turned on.

$$\frac{497 \ words}{reading \ time \ (\qquad) \ sec} \times 60 = (\qquad) \ WPM$$

Build Your Vocabulary

yawn [jɔːn] v. 하품하다; (입·틈 등이) 크게 벌어지다; n. 하품; 따분한 일
If you yawn, you open your mouth very wide and breathe in more air than usual, often when you are tired or are not interested in something.

nap [næp] n. 낮잠; v. (특히 낮에) 잠깐 자다
If you have a nap, you have a short sleep, usually during the day.

sneak up idiom ~에게 몰래 다가가다
If something sneaks up on you, it happens when you are not expecting it.

stretch [stretʃ] v. 기지개를 켜다; 잡아 늘이다; n. (길게) 뻗은 지역; (계속되는) 기간
When you stretch, you put your arms or legs out straight and tighten your muscles.

certain [sə́ːrtn] a. 확실한, 틀림없는; 확신하는 (certainly ad. 분명히)
You use certainly to emphasize what you are saying when you are making a statement.

footstep [fútstep] n. 발소리; 발자국
A footstep is the sound or mark that is made by someone walking each time their foot touches the ground.

odd [ad] a. 이상한, 특이한; 가끔의; 다양한
If you describe someone or something as odd, you think that they are strange or unusual.

be supposed to idiom ~하기로 되어 있다; ~해야 한다
If you say that something is supposed to happen, you mean that it is planned or expected.

handle [hændl] n. 손잡이; v. 다루다, 처리하다; (차량 등이) 말을 잘 듣다
A handle is a small round object or a lever that is attached to a door and is used for opening and closing it.

lock [lak] v. (자물쇠로) 잠그다; 고정시키다; n. 자물쇠
When you lock something such as a door, drawer, or case, you fasten it, usually with a key, so that other people cannot open it.

chime [ʧaim] v. (종이나 시계가) 울리다; 시간을 알리다; n. (차임벨) 소리
When a bell or a clock chimes, it makes ringing sounds.

bong [baŋ] n. 둥, 뎅그렁뎅그렁 (하고 큰 종이 울리는 소리)
A bong is a long, deep sound such as the sound made by a big bell.

count [kaunt] v. (수를) 세다; 계산하다; 포함시키다; n. 셈, 계산; 수치
When you count, you say all the numbers one after another up to a particular number.

distinct [distíŋkt] a. 뚜렷한, 분명한; 구별되는, 별개의 (distinctly ad. 뚜렷하게)
If an idea, thought, or intention is distinct, it is clear and definite.

mention [ménʃən] v. 말하다, 언급하다; n. 언급, 거론
If you mention something, you say something about it, usually briefly.

scare [skɛər] v. 겁주다; 무서워하다; n. 불안; 놀람 (scared a. 무서워하는, 겁먹은)
If you are scared of someone or something, you are frightened of them.

gulp [gʌlp] v. (공포·놀라움에 질려) 침을 꿀떡 삼키다; 꿀꺽꿀꺽 삼키다; n. 꿀꺽 마시기
If you gulp, you swallow air, often making a noise in your throat as you do so, because you are nervous or excited.

familiar [fəmíljər] a. 익숙한, 친숙한; ~에 익숙한
If someone or something is familiar to you, you recognize them or know them well.

nook [nuk] n. (아늑하고 조용한) 구석
A nook is a small and sheltered place.

cranny [krǽni] n. (pl.) (특히 벽에 난 아주 작은) 구멍, 틈
Crannies are very narrow openings or spaces in something.

grab [græb] v. 붙잡다, 움켜잡다; n. 와락 잡아채려고 함
If you grab something, you take it or pick it up suddenly and roughly.

branch [bræntʃ] n. 나뭇가지; 지사, 분점; 부서; v. 갈라지다, 나뉘다
The branches of a tree are the parts that grow out from its trunk and
have leaves, flowers, or fruit growing on them.

blow [blou] v. (blew–blown) (바람·입김에) 날리다; (악기 등을) 불다; 입김을 내뿜다;
n. 바람; 강타
If the wind blows something somewhere or if it blows there, the wind
moves it there.

turn one's back on idiom ~에 등을 돌리다; ~를 외면하다
If you turn your back on someone or something, you turn around very
quickly to face the opposite direction of them.

shelf [ʃelf] n. (pl. shelves) 책꽂이, (책장의) 칸; 선반
A shelf is a flat piece which is attached to a wall or to the sides of a
cupboard for keeping things on.

squeeze [skwi:z] v. (꼭) 짜다, 쥐다; (좁은 곳에) 밀어 넣다; n. 짜기
(squeeze one's eyes shut idiom 눈을 꼭 감다)
If you squeeze your eyes shut or if your eyes squeeze shut, you close
them tightly, usually because you are frightened or to protect your eyes
from something such as strong sunlight.

calm [ka:m] a. 침착한, 차분한; 잔잔한; v. 진정시키다; n. 평온; 진정
A calm person does not show or feel any worry, anger, or excitement.

mind one's own business idiom 남의 일에 간섭하지 않다
If you mind your own business, you concern yourself only with what is
of interest to yourself and do not interfere in the affairs of others.

stack [stæk] n. (pl.) (도서관의) 서가; 무더기, 더미; v. 쌓다, 포개다; 채우다
The stacks refer to storage space in a library consisting of an extensive arrangement of bookshelves where most of the books are stored.

crash [kræʃ] n. 요란한 소리; (자동차·항공기) 사고; v. 부딪치다; 충돌하다; 굉음을 내다
A crash is a sudden, loud noise.

imagination [imædʒənéiʃən] n. 상상력, 상상; 착각; 창의력
Your imagination is the ability that you have to form pictures or ideas in your mind of things that are new and exciting, or things that you have not experienced.

make up idiom (이야기 등을) 만들어 내다; ~을 이루다, 형성하다
If you make up something, you invent something artificial or untrue, often in order to trick someone.

bite [bait] v. (bit–bitten) (이빨로) 물다; n. 물기; 한 입
If you bite something, you use your teeth to cut into it, for example in order to eat it or break it.

pound [paund] v. (가슴·피가) 쿵쿵 뛰다; 세게 치다; n. 타격; 두들기는 소리
If your heart is pounding, it is beating with an unusually strong and fast rhythm, usually because you are afraid.

chest [tʃest] ① n. 가슴, 흉부 ② n. 상자, 궤
Your chest is the top part of the front of your body where your ribs, lungs, and heart are.

creak [kriːk] v. 삐걱거리다; n. 삐걱거리는 소리
If something creaks, it makes a short, high-pitched sound when it moves.

sneaker [sníːkər] n. (pl.) 운동화
Sneakers are casual shoes with rubber soles.

reach [riːtʃ] v. 이르다, 도달하다; (손·팔을) 뻗다, 내밀다; n. 거리; 범위
When someone or something reaches a place, they arrive there.

scary [skέəri] a. 무서운, 겁나는
Something that is scary is rather frightening.

‡ arm [ɑːrm] v. 무장하다; n. 팔; (pl.) 무기 (armed a. 무기를 소지한)
Someone who is armed is carrying a weapon, usually a gun.

‡ battle [bætl] n. 전투; 투쟁; 싸움; v. 싸우다, 투쟁하다
A battle is a violent fight between groups of people, especially one
between military forces during a war.

＊ sharpen [ʃɑ́ːrpən] v. (날카롭게) 깎다; 날카롭게 하다; 더 강렬해지다
If you sharpen an object, you make its edge very thin or you make its
end pointed.

‡ further [fə́ːrðər] a. 더 이상의, 추가의; ad. 더; 더 멀리에; v. 발전시키다
A further thing, number of things, or amount of something is an
additional thing, number of things, or amount.

fluke [fluːk] n. 요행(수), 우연한 사건
If you say that something good is a fluke, you mean that it happened
accidentally rather than by being planned or arranged.

‡ pile [pail] n. 쌓아 놓은 것; 더미, 무더기; v. 쌓다, 포개다; (많은 사람들이) 우르르 가다
A pile of things is a quantity of things that have been put neatly
somewhere so that each thing is on top of the one below.

‡ relax [rilǽks] v. 안심하다, 진정하다; 휴식을 취하다; 긴장을 풀다
If you relax or if something relaxes you, you feel more calm and less
worried.

‡ concentrate [kánsəntrèit] v. (정신을) 집중하다; 농축하다; n. 농축물
If you concentrate on something, you give all your attention to it.

Chapter 6

1. **Why did Francine scream?**

   A. She was afraid of Arthur.

   B. She wanted to surprise Arthur.

   C. She wanted to scare Arthur.

   D. Arthur had screamed first.

2. **What had caused the crash?**

   A. Francine had accidentally set off the library's security alarm.

   B. Francine had accidentally knocked some books off a desk.

   C. Francine had tried to open the locked door.

   D. Francine had thrown a book at the locked door.

3. Why did Francine blame Arthur for getting them locked in the library?

A. Arthur was supposed to have come find her.

B. Arthur was supposed to have taken a shorter nap.

C. Arthur was supposed to have talked to Ms. Turner.

D. Arthur was supposed to have found more books.

4. Why had Francine not heard the clock?

A. She had been too interested in reading her book.

B. She had been talking with Ms. Turner.

C. She had been listening to music.

D. She had been in the bathroom.

5. How did Francine feel about her plan to escape from the library?

A. She already had a plan ready to put into operation with Arthur's help.

B. She thought that it was going to be really hard to escape.

C. She was working on a plan and needed Arthur's ideas.

D. She was working on a plan but wouldn't share it with Arthur.

$$\frac{413 \ words}{reading \ time \ (\qquad) \ sec} \times 60 = (\qquad) \ WPM$$

Build Your Vocabulary

* **whirl** [hwə:rl] v. 빙그르르 돌다; n. 빙빙 돌기, 선회하기
  If something or someone whirls around or if you whirl them around, they move around or turn around very quickly.

* **breath** [breθ] n. 숨, 입김 (take a deep breath idiom 심호흡하다)
  When you take a deep breath, you breathe in a lot of air at one time.

* **crash** [kræʃ] n. 요란한 소리; (자동차·항공기) 사고; v. 부딪치다; 충돌하다; 쾅음을 내다
  A crash is a sudden, loud noise.

* **accidental** [æksədéntl] a. 우연한, 돌발적인 (accidentally ad. 우연히, 뜻하지 않게)
  An accidental event happens by chance or as the result of an accident, and is not deliberately intended.

* **knock** [nak] v. 치다; 부딪치다; (문을) 두드리다; n. 문 두드리는 소리; 부딪침
  If you knock something, you touch or hit it roughly, especially so that it falls or moves.

* **barely** [béərli] ad. 거의 ~아니게; 간신히, 가까스로, 빠듯하게
  You use barely to say that something is only just true or only just the case.

* **insist** [insíst] v. 고집하다, 주장하다, 우기다
  If you insist that something is the case, you say so very firmly and refuse to say otherwise, even though other people do not believe you.

investigate [invéstəgèit] v. 조사하다, 수사하다, 살피다
If someone, especially an official, investigates an event, situation, or claim, they try to find out what happened or what is the truth.

creepy [krí:pi] a. 오싹하게 하는, 으스스한; (섬뜩할 정도로) 기이한
If you say that something or someone is creepy, you mean they make you feel very nervous or frightened.

frown [fraun] n. 찡그림, 찌푸림; v. 얼굴을 찌푸리다
A frown is a facial expression or look characterized by a furrowing of one's brows.

hip [hip] n. 허리; 둔부, 엉덩이
Your hips are the two areas at the sides of your body between the tops of your legs and your waist.

sigh [sai] v. 한숨을 쉬다, 한숨짓다; n. 한숨; 탄식
When you sigh, you let out a deep breath, as a way of expressing feelings such as disappointment, tiredness, or pleasure.

chime [ʧaim] v. (종이나 시계가) 울리다; 시간을 알리다; n. (차임벨) 소리
When a bell or a clock chimes, it makes ringing sounds.

count [kaunt] v. (수를) 세다; 계산하다; 포함시키다; n. 셈, 계산; 수치
When you count, you say all the numbers one after another up to a particular number.

impress [imprés] v. 깊은 인상을 주다, 감명을 주다; 새기다 (impressed a. 감명을 받은)
If something impresses you, you feel great admiration for it.

lock [lak] v. (자물쇠로) 잠그다; 고정시키다; n. 자물쇠 (lock in idiom ~을 가두다)
If you lock something or someone in a place, room, or container, you put them there and fasten the lock.

blush [blʌʃ] v. 얼굴을 붉히다; ~에 부끄러워하다; n. 얼굴이 붉어짐
When you blush, your face becomes redder than usual because you are ashamed or embarrassed.

hesitate [hézətèit] v. 망설이다, 주저하다
If you hesitate, you do not speak or act for a short time, usually because you are uncertain, embarrassed, or worried about what you are going to say or do.

silly [síli] a. 어리석은, 바보 같은; 유치한; n. 바보
If you say that someone or something is silly, you mean that they are foolish, childish, or ridiculous.

make a face idiom 얼굴을 찌푸리다; 침울한 표정을 짓다
If you make a face, you show a feeling such as dislike or disgust by putting an exaggerated expression on your face.

excuse [ikskjúːz] n. 핑계 거리; 변명, 이유; v. 용서하다
An excuse is a reason which you give in order to explain why something has been done or has not been done, or in order to avoid doing something.

attention [əténʃən] n. 주의, 주목; 관심 (**pay attention** idiom 주의를 기울이다)
If you pay attention to someone, you watch them, listen to them, or take notice of them.

never mind idiom (중요하지 않으니까) 신경 쓰지 마, 괜찮아
You use 'never mind' to tell someone not to do something or worry about something, because it is not important.

argue [áːrgjuː] v. 언쟁을 하다; 주장하다
If one person argues with another, they speak angrily to each other about something that they disagree about.

work on idiom (해결하기 위해) ~에 애쓰다; (원하는) 효과가 나다
If you say 'I'm working on it,' you mean that you are dealing with it.

sniff [snif] v. 콧방귀를 뀌다; 코를 훌쩍이다; n. 콧방귀 뀌기
You can use sniff to indicate that someone says something in a way that shows their disapproval or contempt.

put into operation idiom ~을 실시하다
When a rule, system, or plan comes into operation or you put it into operation, you begin to use it.

make the point idiom 주장하다, 강조하다; 요점을 말하다
If you make the point, you prove that something is true, either by arguing about it or by your actions or behavior.

stick [stik] v. (stuck–stuck) 찔러 넣다; 고수하다; 꼼짝하지 않다; n. 막대
If you stick something somewhere, you put it there in a rather casual way.

Chapter 7

1. **What idea did Arthur and Francine both have for what to do next?**

   A. They both thought that they could try to find the keys to the front door.

   B. They both thought that they could try to escape through the window.

   C. They both thought that they could find the emergency exit.

   D. They both thought that they could try to call home.

2. **How did Francine lose her balance when she was standing on the pile of books?**

   A. Arthur took a book from the bottom of the pile.

   B. Arthur accidentally bumped into the pile.

   C. Francine waved her hand wildly at a fly.

   D. Francine had made a rickety pile of books.

3. What was the source of the growling sound?

   A. An electric generator for the library

   B. A refrigerator in the library

   C. A monster in the library

   D. Arthur's stomach

4. What book did Francine look up?

   A. A phone book for the city

   B. How to Escape from a Library

   C. How to Survive a Night in a Library

   D. How to Find Food in a Library

5. How did Francine feel about the book being missing?

   A. She thought that it was a cruel joke.

   B. She felt that it had never really been there.

   C. She thought that nobody would need it outside of a library.

   D. She felt that Arthur had taken and hidden it somewhere else.

1분에 몇 단어를 읽는지 리딩 속도를 측정해보세요.

$$\frac{513 \text{ words}}{\text{reading time ( ) sec}} \times 60 = (\qquad) \text{ WPM}$$

Build Your Vocabulary

^{복습} **pile** [pail] v. 쌓다, 포개다; (많은 사람들이) 우르르 가다; n. 쌓아 놓은 것; 더미, 무더기
If you pile things somewhere, you put them there so that they form a pile.

rickety [ríkiti] a. 곧 무너질 듯한, 흔들흔들하는
A rickety structure or piece of furniture is not very strong or well made, and seems likely to collapse or break.

＊ **sway** [swei] v. 흔들리다; (마음을) 흔들다; n. 흔들림, 진동
When people or things sway, they lean or swing slowly from one side to the other.

^{복습} **back and forth** [bæk ən fɔ́ːrθ] idiom 앞뒤로; 좌우로; 여기저기에, 왔다 갔다
If someone moves back and forth, they repeatedly move in one direction and then in the opposite direction.

be about to idiom 막 ~하려는 참이다
If you are about to do something, you are going to do it immediately.

^{복습} **grab** [græb] v. 붙잡다, 움켜잡다; n. 와락 잡아채려고 함
If you grab something, you take it or pick it up suddenly and roughly.

^{복습} **handle** [hǽndl] n. 손잡이; v. 다루다, 처리하다; (차량 등이) 말을 잘 듣다
A handle is a small round object or a lever that is attached to a door and is used for opening and closing it.

come by idiom 잠깐 들르다
If you come by somewhere, you visit a place for a short time, often when you are going somewhere else.

exact [igzǽkt] a. 정확한, 정밀한; 엄격한 (exactly ad. 정확히, 틀림없이; 맞아)
You use exactly before an amount, number, or position to emphasize that it is no more, no less, or no different from what you are stating.

neat [niːt] a. 정돈된, 단정한; 깔끔한
A neat place, thing, or person is tidy and smart, and has everything in the correct place.

yank [jæŋk] v. 홱 잡아당기다; n. 홱 잡아당기기
If you yank someone or something somewhere, you pull them there suddenly and with a lot of force.

thud [θʌd] n. 쿵, 퍽 (하고 무거운 것이 떨어지는 소리); v. 쿵 하고 치다
A thud is a dull sound, such as that a heavy object makes when it hits something soft.

in place idiom 제자리에 있는; ~을 위한 준비가 되어 있는
If something is in place, it is prepared and ready.

steady [stédi] a. 흔들림 없는, 안정된; 꾸준한; v. 흔들리지 않다, 진정되다
If an object is steady, it is firm and does not shake or move about.

give a pull idiom ~을 잡아당기다
If you give something a pull, you hold it firmly and use force in order to move it toward you or away from its previous position.

latch [læʧ] n. 걸쇠; 자물쇠; v. 걸쇠를 걸다, 걸쇠로 잠그다
A latch is a fastening on a door or gate. It consists of a metal bar which you lift in order to open the door.

stick [stik] v. 꼼짝하지 않다; 찔러 넣다; 고수하다; n. 막대 (stuck a. 꼼짝 못하는; 갇힌)
If something is stuck in a particular position, it is fixed tightly in this position and is unable to move.

tug [tʌg] n. 잡아당김; v. (세게) 잡아당기다; 끌어당기다 (**give a tug** idiom 홱 끌어당기다)
If you give something a tug, you pull it hard or suddenly.

buzz [bʌz] v. 윙윙거리다; 부산스럽다; n. 윙윙거리는 소리; 웅성거림
If something buzzes or buzzes somewhere, it makes a long continuous
sound, like the noise a bee makes when it is flying.

wave [weiv] v. 흔들다; 손짓하다; n. (팔·손·몸을) 흔들기; 파도, 물결
If you wave or wave your hand, you move your hand from side to side
in the air, usually in order to say hello or goodbye to someone.

land [lænd] v. 떨어지다; 내려앉다, 착륙하다; n. 육지; 땅, 지역
When someone or something lands, they come down to the ground
after moving through the air or falling.

crash [kræʃ] n. 요란한 소리; (자동차·항공기) 사고; v. 부딪치다; 충돌하다; 굉음을 내다
A crash is a sudden, loud noise.

trip [trip] v. 발을 헛디디다; ~를 넘어뜨리다; n. 여행; 발을 헛디딤
If you trip when you are walking, you knock your foot against something
and fall or nearly fall.

pick oneself up idiom (넘어졌다가) 일어서다
If you pick yourself up, you stand up again after a fall.

balance [bǽləns] n. 균형, 평형; v. 균형을 유지하다; 균형을 이루다
Balance is the ability to remain steady when you are standing up.

forget it idiom 생각도 하지 마; 잊어버려, 별 거 아냐
If you say 'forget it' to someone, you tell them not to worry or bother
about something, or say no to a suggestion emphatically.

snap [snæp] v. (화난 목소리로) 딱딱거리다; 딱 (하고) 움직이다; n. 찰칵 하는 소리
If someone snaps at you, they speak to you in a sharp, unfriendly way.

gulp [gʌlp] v. (공포·놀라움에 질려) 침을 꿀떡 삼키다; 꿀꺽꿀꺽 삼키다; n. 꿀꺽 마시기
If you gulp, you swallow air, often making a noise in your throat as you
do so, because you are nervous or excited.

growl [graul] v. 으르렁거리다; 으르렁거리듯 말하다; n. 으르렁거리는 소리
When a dog or other animal growls, it makes a low noise in its throat, usually because it is angry.

stomach [stʌ́mək] n. 복부; 배
Your stomach is the organ inside your body where food is digested before it moves into the intestines.

poster [póustər] n. (벽에 붙이는) 대형 그림; (안내·홍보용) 포스터
A poster is a large notice or picture that you stick on a wall or board, often in order to advertise something.

throw out idiom (더 이상 필요 없는 것을) 버리다, 없애다
If you throw something out, you get rid of something that has no use or that you no longer need.

catalog [kǽtəlɔ̀ːg] n. (상품·자료의) 목록, 카탈로그; v. 목록을 작성하다
A catalog is a list of things such as the goods you can buy from a particular company, the objects in a museum, or the books in a library.

flip through idiom ~을 훑어보다, 휙휙 넘기다
If you flip through something such as a book, you turn over the pages of a book quickly without reading everything.

listing [lístiŋ] n. 일람표, 목록, 명단
A listing is a published list, or an item in a published list.

ignore [ignɔ́ːr] v. 무시하다; (사람을) 못 본 척하다
If you ignore someone or something, you pay no attention to them.

prison [prizn] n. 교도소, 감옥
A prison is a building where criminals are kept as punishment or where people accused of a crime are kept.

desert island [dèzərt áilənd] n. (열대의) 무인도
A desert island is a small tropical island, where nobody lives.

impress [imprés] v. 깊은 인상을 주다, 감명을 주다; 새기다 (impressed a. 감명을 받은)
If something impresses you, you feel great admiration for it.

realize [ríːəlàiz] v. 깨닫다, 알아차리다; 실현하다
If you realize that something is true, you become aware of that fact or understand it.

sort [sɔːrt] n. 종류, 유형; v. 분류하다, 구분하다
If you talk about a particular sort of something, you are talking about a class of things that have particular features in common.

stack [stæk] n. (pl.) (도서관의) 서가; 무더기, 더미; v. 쌓다, 포개다; 채우다
The stacks refer to storage space in a library consisting of an extensive arrangement of bookshelves where most of the books are stored.

gap [gæp] n. 틈, 구멍; 공백; 격차
A gap is a space between two things or a hole in the middle of something solid.

Chapter 8

1. Who called the library?

   A. Francine's father

   B. Ms. Turner

   C. Buster

   D. Muffy

2. Why could Arthur and Francine not use the phone to call outside of the library?

   A. The power was out.

   B. It needed a user code.

   C. There was no connection.

   D. They had used up their minutes.

3. What did Arthur do with the magazine?

A. He gave it to Francine to calm her down.

B. He used it for a pillow while he took a nap.

C. He used it to distract himself from being scared.

D. He ripped out a photo of a roast turkey and chewed it.

4. Why did Arthur go searching for Francine?

A. He finally wanted to apologize to her.

B. He wanted to share an idea for their escape plan.

C. He heard screams and was worried about Francine.

D. He was afraid of being all alone in the library.

5. What was behind the first door that Arthur opened?

A. A toilet

B. A broom closet

C. A pile of books

D. A study room

1분에 몇 단어를 읽는지 리딩 속도를 측정해보세요.

$$\frac{533 \text{ words}}{\text{reading time ( ) sec}} \times 60 = (\qquad) \text{ WPM}$$

Build Your Vocabulary

somehow [sΛ́mhàu] ad. 왜 그런지 (모르겠지만), 왠지
You use somehow to say that you do not know or cannot say how something was done or will be done.

freeze [fri:z] v. (두려움 등으로 몸이) 얼어붙다; 얼다; 얼리다; n. 동결
(frozen a. (몸이) 얼어붙은)
If someone who is moving freezes, they suddenly stop and become completely still and quiet.

race [reis] v. 쏜살같이 가다; 경쟁하다, 경주하다; n. 경주; 인종, 민족
If you race somewhere, you go there as quickly as possible.

grab [græb] v. 붙잡다, 움켜잡다; n. 와락 잡아채려고 함
If you grab something, you take it or pick it up suddenly and roughly.

receive [risíːv] v. 수신하다; 받다, 받아들이다 (receiver n. 수화기)
A telephone's receiver is the part that you hold near to your ear and speak into.

on the line idiom 전화선에, 전화상으로
If you are on the line with someone, you speak to them on the telephone.

cut in idiom (말·대화에) 끼어들다, (남의 말을) 자르다
If you cut in on someone or their conversation, you interrupt them while they are speaking.

lock [lak] v. (자물쇠로) 잠그다; 고정시키다; n. 자물쇠 (lock in idiom ~을 가두다)
If you lock something or someone in a place, room, or container, you put them there and fasten the lock.

dial [dáiəl] v. 다이얼을 돌리다, 전화를 걸다; n. (시계·계기 등의) 문자반
If you dial, you turn the dial or press the buttons on a telephone in order to phone someone.

hang up idiom 전화를 끊다, 수화기를 놓다
If you hang up the phone, you end a telephone conversation, often very suddenly.

stare [stɛər] v. 빤히 쳐다보다, 응시하다; n. 빤히 쳐다보기, 응시
If you stare at someone or something, you look at them for a long time.

relax [rilǽks] v. 안심하다, 진정하다; 휴식을 취하다; 긴장을 풀다
If you relax or if something relaxes you, you feel more calm and less worried.

beep [bi:p] n. 삑 하는 소리; v. 삐 소리를 내다; (경적을) 울리다
A beep is a short, loud sound like that made by a car horn or a telephone answering machine.

recording [rikɔ́:rdiŋ] n. 녹음(된 것); 기록
A recording of something is a record, CD, tape, or video of it.

code [koud] n. 암호, 부호; 규칙; v. 암호로 쓰다 (user code n. 사용자 고유 번호)
A code is a group of numbers or letters which is used to identify something, such as a postal address or part of a telephone system.

slam [slæm] v. 세게 놓다; 쾅 닫다; n. 탕 하는 소리
If you slam something down, you put it there quickly and with great force.

come to idiom (좋지 않은 상황이) 되다
To come to something means to reach a particular state or point, especially a bad or unpleasant one.

doom [du:m] v. 불행한 운명을 맞게 하다; n. 죽음, 파멸 (**doomed** a. 운이 다한, 불운한)
If something is doomed to happen, or if you are doomed to a particular state, something unpleasant is certain to happen, and you can do nothing to prevent it.

wimp [wimp] n. 겁쟁이, 약골
If you call someone a wimp, you disapprove of them because they lack confidence or determination, or because they are often afraid of things.

bossy [bási] a. 우두머리 행세를 하는, 으스대는
If you describe someone as bossy, you mean that they enjoy telling people what to do.

know-it-all [nóu-it-ɔ́:l] a. 아는 체하는, 똑똑한 체하는; n. 아는 체하는 사람
If you say that someone is a know-it-all, you are critical of them because they think that they know a lot more than other people.

that does it idiom 더 이상은 못 참아
You can say 'That does it' to show that you will not tolerate something any longer.

storm [stɔ:rm] v. (화가 나서) 쿵쾅대며 가다, 뛰쳐나가다; n. 폭풍, 폭풍우
If you storm into or out of a place, you enter or leave it quickly and noisily, because you are angry.

deepen [dí:pən] v. (색이) 짙어지다; (감정 등이) 깊어지다
If a color deepens, it becomes darker.

gloom [glu:m] n. 어둠; 우울, 침울
The gloom is a state of near darkness.

flip through idiom ~을 훑어보다, 휙휙 넘기다
If you flip through something such as a book, you turn over the pages of a book quickly without reading everything.

roast [roust] a. 구운; v. 굽다; 볶다; n. 구운 고기, 구이 요리
Roast meat has been cooked by roasting.

turkey [tə́:rki] n. 칠면조 (고기)
A turkey is a large bird that is kept on a farm for its meat.

stomach [stʌ́mək] n. 복부; 배
Your stomach is the organ inside your body where food is digested before it moves into the intestines.

grumble [grʌmbl] v. 우르릉거리다; 투덜거리다; n. 불평; 우르릉거리는 소리
If something grumbles, it makes a low continuous sound.

mutter [mʌ́tər] v. 중얼거리다; 투덜거리다; n. 중얼거림
If you mutter, you speak very quietly so that you cannot easily be heard, often because you are complaining about something.

rip [rip] v. 찢다; 떼어 내다, 뜯어 내다; n. 찢어진 곳
When something rips or when you rip it, you tear it forcefully with your hands or with a tool such as a knife.

chew [ʧuː] v. (음식을) 씹다; 물어뜯다; n. 씹기, 깨물기
When you chew food, you use your teeth to break it up in your mouth so that it becomes easier to swallow.

yuck [jʌk] int. 윽 (하고 역겨울 때 내는 소리)
'Yuck' is an expression of disgust.

spit [spit] v. (침·음식물 등을) 뱉다; (욕·폭언 등을) 내뱉다; n. 침
If you spit liquid or food somewhere, you force a small amount of it out of your mouth.

thump [θʌmp] n. 쿵 하는 소리; v. (세게) 치다; 쿵 하고 떨어지다
A thump is a loud, dull sound by hitting something.

frown [fraun] v. 얼굴을 찌푸리다; n. 찡그림, 찌푸림
When someone frowns, their eyebrows become drawn together, because they are annoyed or puzzled.

be supposed to idiom ~하기로 되어 있다; ~해야 한다
If you say that something is supposed to happen, you mean that it is planned or expected.

wonder [wʌ́ndər] v. 궁금해하다; (크게) 놀라다; n. 경탄, 경이
If you wonder about something, you think about it because it interests you and you want to know more about it.

mash [mæʃ] v. (음식을 부드럽게) 으깨다; n. 으깨 놓은 것
If you mash food that is solid but soft, you crush it so that it forms a soft mass.

echo [ékou] v. (소리가) 울리다, 메아리 치다; n. 울림, 메아리
If a sound echoes, it is reflected off a surface and can be heard again after the original sound has stopped.

hall [hɔːl] n. (건물 안의) 복도; 현관; 넓은 방, 홀
A hall in a building is a long passage with doors into rooms on both sides of it.

broom [bruːm] n. 비, 빗자루
A broom is a kind of brush with a long handle.

closet [klázit] n. 벽장
A closet is a piece of furniture with doors at the front and shelves inside, which is used for storing things.

evil [íːvəl] a. 사악한, 악랄한; 악마의; n. 악
If you describe something as evil, you mean that you think it causes a great deal of harm to people and is morally bad.

laughter [lǽftər] n. 웃음소리; 웃음, 웃기
Laughter is the sound of people laughing, for example because they are amused or happy.

waste [weist] v. (돈·시간 등을) 낭비하다; 헛되이 쓰다; n. 낭비; 쓰레기
If you waste something such as time, money, or energy, you use too much of it doing something that is not important or necessary, or is unlikely to succeed.

breath [breθ] n. 숨, 입김 (take a deep breath idiom 심호흡하다)
When you take a deep breath, you breathe in a lot of air at one time.

burst [bəːrst] v. 불쑥 움직이다; 터지다, 파열하다; n. (갑자기) 한바탕 ~을 함

To burst into or out of a place means to enter or leave it suddenly with a lot of energy or force.

Chapter 9

1. **What happened as Arthur entered the room?**

   A. He was attacked by a monster.

   B. He was startled by Francine.

   C. He tripped on a pizza box and hit his head.

   D. He tripped on the rug and dropped his glasses.

2. **What was the source of the thumping, screaming, and evil laughter?**

   A. Francine's Walkman

   B. The library's sound system

   C. A horror movie on TV

   D. Francine reading a book out loud

3. Why was there a TV and pizza in the room?

   A. It was a study room for honors students.

   B. It was the staff room for the librarians.

   C. It was the break room for the teachers.

   D. It was Ms. Turner's private office.

4. How did Francine react to Arthur saying that he was coming to her rescue?

   A. She told him that she didn't want his help.

   B. She told him that he could have been hurt.

   C. She told him to go find his own pizza.

   D. She told him that he was brave.

5. What happened after Arthur and Francine finished eating the pizza and snacks?

   A. D.W., Arthur's father, Francine's mother, and Ms. Turner found them in the library.

   B. They napped and dreamed that Arthur's father and Francine's mother came to get them.

   C. Ms. Turner got angry at them for eating staff's food.

   D. Arthur's father called the library.

1분에 몇 단어를 읽는지 리딩 속도를 측정해보세요.

$$\frac{514 \text{ words}}{\text{reading time ( ) sec}} \times 60 = (\quad) \text{ WPM}$$

Build Your Vocabulary

trip [trip] v. 발을 헛디디다; ~를 넘어뜨리다; n. 여행; 발을 헛디딤
If you trip when you are walking, you knock your foot against something and fall or nearly fall.

rug [rʌg] n. 깔개, 양탄자
A rug is a piece of thick material that you put on a floor.

sail [seil] v. 미끄러지듯 나아가다; 항해하다; n. 돛; 항해
If a person or thing sails somewhere, they move there smoothly and fairly quickly.

land [lænd] v. 떨어지다; 내려앉다, 착륙하다; n. 육지; 땅, 지역
When someone or something lands, they come down to the ground after moving through the air or falling.

squint [skwint] v. 눈을 가늘게 뜨고 보다; n. 사시
If you squint at something, you look at it with your eyes partly closed.

scramble [skræmbl] v. 재빨리 움직이다; (달걀을 휘저어) 스크램블을 만들다; n. (힘들게) 기어가기
If you scramble to a different place or position, you move there in a hurried, awkward way.

strand [strænd] n. (실·전선·머리카락 등의) 가닥, 줄; v. 오도 가도 못 하게 하다
A strand of something such as hair, wire, or thread is a single thin piece of it.

dangle [dǽŋgl] v. 매달리다; 매달리게 들다
If something dangles from somewhere or if you dangle it somewhere, it hangs or swings loosely.

⋆ **lens** [lenz] n. 렌즈; (안구의) 수정체
A lens is a thin curved piece of glass or plastic used in things such as cameras, telescopes, and pairs of glasses.

⋆ **wipe** [waip] v. (먼지·물기 등을) 닦다; 지우다; n. 닦기, 훔치기
If you wipe something, you rub its surface to remove dirt or liquid from it.

복습 **thump** [θʌmp] v. 쿵 하고 떨어지다; (세게) 치다; n. 쿵 하는 소리
If you thump something somewhere or if it thumps there, it makes a loud, dull sound by hitting something else.

⋆ **monster** [mánstər] n. (이야기 속의) 괴물; a. 기이하게 큰, 거대한
A monster is a large imaginary creature that looks very ugly and frightening.

⋆ **horror** [hɔ́ːrər] n. (책·영화 등) 공포물; 공포(감), 경악
A horror film or story is intended to be very frightening.

복습 **evil** [íːvəl] a. 사악한, 악랄한; 악마의; n. 악
If you describe something as evil, you mean that you think it causes a great deal of harm to people and is morally bad.

복습 **go on** idiom 말을 계속하다; (어떤 상황이) 계속되다; 시작하다
When you go on, you continue speaking after a short pause.

⋆⋆ **strange** [streindʒ] a. 이상한; 낯선
Something that is strange is unusual or unexpected, and makes you feel slightly nervous or afraid.

⋆⋆ **humor** [hjúːmər] n. 유머러스함; 익살; v. 비위를 맞춰 주다
Someone who has a sense of humor often finds things amusing, rather than being serious all the time.

figure [fígjər] v. 생각하다, 판단하다; 중요하다; n. 수치; (멀리서 흐릿하게 보이는) 모습
If you figure that something is the case, you think or guess that it is the case.

rescue [réskju:] n. 구출, 구조; 구출 작업; v. 구하다, 구조하다, 구출하다
(come to one's rescue idiom ~을 구하기 위해 오다)
If you come to someone's rescue, you help them when they are in danger or difficulty.

shrug [ʃrʌg] v. (어깨를) 으쓱하다; n. (어깨를) 으쓱하기
If you shrug, you raise your shoulders to show that you are not interested in something or that you do not know or care about something.

staff [stæf] n. 직원; v. 직원으로 일하다
The staff of an organization are the people who work for it.

librarian [laibréəriən] n. (도서관의) 사서
A librarian is a person who is in charge of a library or who has been specially trained to work in a library.

feed [fi:d] v. (fed-fed) 먹이다; 먹이를 주다; n. (동식물의) 먹이
If you feed a person or animal, you give them food to eat and sometimes actually put it in their mouths.

refrigerator [rifrídʒərèitər] n. 냉장고
A refrigerator is a large container which is kept cool inside, usually by electricity, so that the food and drink in it stays fresh.

zap [zæp] v. 전자레인지로 요리하다; 재빠르게 하다, 해치우다
To zap something means to heat or cook it in a microwave oven.

microwave [máikrouwèiv] n. (= microwave oven) 전자레인지; v. 전자레인지에 요리하다
A microwave or a microwave oven is an oven which cooks food very quickly by electromagnetic radiation rather than by heat.

get straight idiom 분명히 하다; ~을 명쾌하게 이해하다
If you get something straight, you make sure that you understand it properly or that someone else does.

stick [stik] v. 꼼짝하지 않다; 찔러 넣다; 고수하다; n. 막대 (stuck a. 갇힌; 꼼짝 못하는)
If you are stuck in a place, you want to get away from it but are unable to.

nod [nad] v. (고개를) 끄덕이다, 끄덕여 나타내다; n. (고개를) 끄덕임
If you nod, you move your head downward and upward to show agreement, understanding, or approval.

bet [bet] v. 틀림없다, 분명하다; (내기 등에) 돈을 걸다; n. 내기; 짐작
You use expressions such as 'I bet,' 'I'll bet,' and 'you can bet' to indicate that you are sure something is true.

resourceful [risɔ́:rsfəl] a. 임기응변의 재주가 있는, 재치 있는
Someone who is resourceful is good at finding ways of dealing with problems.

be about to idiom 막 ~하려는 참이다
If you are about to do something, you are going to do it immediately.

admit [ædmít] v. 인정하다, 시인하다
If you admit that something bad, unpleasant, or embarrassing is true, you agree, often unwillingly, that it is true.

stomach [stʌ́mək] n. 복부; 배
Your stomach is the organ inside your body where food is digested before it moves into the intestines.

grumble [grʌmbl] v. 우르릉거리다; 투덜거리다; n. 불평; 우르릉거리는 소리
If something grumbles, it makes a low continuous sound.

consider [kənsídər] v. 고려하다, 숙고하다; 여기다
If you consider something, you think about it carefully.

ancient [éinʃənt] a. 아주 오래된; 고대의
Ancient means very old, or having existed for a long time.

history [hístəri] n. 역사; 역사(학)
If you say that an event, thing, or person is history, you mean that they are no longer important.

pause [pɔːz] v. (말·일을 하다가) 잠시 멈추다; 정지시키다; n. 멈춤
If you pause while you are doing something, you stop for a short period and then continue.

sort of idiom 어느 정도, 다소; 말하자면
You use sort of when you want to say that your description of something is not very accurate.

plate [pleit] n. 접시, 그릇; (자동차) 번호판; 판, 패 v. 판을 대다
A plate is a round or oval flat dish that is used to hold food.

pleased [pliːzd] a. 기쁜, 기뻐하는, 만족해하는
If you are pleased, you are happy about something or satisfied with something.

sit back idiom (의자에) 편안히 앉다
If you sit back, you sit comfortably with your back against the back of a chair.

groan [groun] v. 신음 소리를 내다, 끙끙거리다; n. 신음, 끙 하는 소리
If you groan, you make a long, low sound because you are in pain, or because you are upset or unhappy about something.

package [pǽkidʒ] n. (포장용) 상자; 포장물; v. 포장하다
A package is a small container in which a quantity of something is sold.

chip [ʧip] n. 감자 칩; 조각, 부스러기; v. 이가 빠지다; 깎다
Chips are long, thin pieces of potato fried in oil or fat and eaten hot, usually with a meal.

scatter [skǽtər] v. 흩뿌리다; 황급히 흩어지다; n. 흩뿌림; 소수
If you scatter things over an area, you throw or drop them so that they spread all over the area.

turn out idiom (일이) ~으로 되어가다; ~으로 밝혀지다
If things turn out, they take place or happen in the way mentioned or develop or end in a particular way.

expect [ikspékt] v. 예상하다, 기대하다; 요구하다
If you expect something to happen, you believe that it will happen.

chore [tʃɔːr] n. (pl.) (가정의) 잡일, 허드렛일; 따분한 일
Chores are tasks such as cleaning, washing, and ironing that have to be done regularly at home.

appear [əpíər] v. 나타나다, 보이기 시작하다; ~인 것 같다
When someone or something appears, they move into a position where you can see them.

doorway [dɔ́ːrwèi] n. 출입구; 현관
A doorway is a space in a wall where a door opens and closes.

thank goodness idiom 정말 다행이다
You say 'thank God' or 'thank goodness' when you are very relieved about something.

survive [sərváiv] v. 살아남다, 생존하다; 견뎌 내다
If a person or living thing survives in a dangerous situation such as an accident or an illness, they do not die.

Chapter 10

1. **Why were people crowding around Arthur and Francine on Monday morning?**

   A. They wanted to hear their report.

   B. They missed them over the weekend.

   C. They wanted to hear the full story about being locked in the library.

   D. They wanted to hear about their punishment from breaking into the library.

2. **What did Binky think happened after the library closed?**

   A. He thought that ghosts came out to scare people.

   B. He thought that the characters in books came out to play.

   C. He thought that the librarians ate pizza and watched TV.

   D. He thought that the librarians stayed to protect the books.

3. What happened to Arthur and Francine's report on Joan of Arc?

A. They had forgotten to do it.

B. They had finished it together after they left the library.

C. They had finished it all during their time in the library.

D. They asked Mr. Ratburn for a different project.

4. How did Mr. Ratburn react to Arthur and Francine's presentation?

A. He thought that they deserved an A.

B. He thought that they should choose another hero.

C. He thought that their experience was better than a report.

D. He thought that their adventure would give their report special meaning.

5. What did Francine do while Arthur and Buster were walking home?

A. She splattered them with mud from a puddle.

B. She offered to help them carry their books home.

C. She wanted to walk home together with them.

D. She offered them a ride in her father's truck.

1분에 몇 단어를 읽는지 리딩 속도를 측정해보세요.

$$\frac{479 \ words}{reading \ time \ (\quad) \ sec} \times 60 = (\quad) \ WPM$$

Build Your Vocabulary

crowd [kraud] v. 가득 메우다; (생각이 마음속에) 밀려오다; n. 사람들, 군중, 무리
When people crowd around someone or something, they gather closely together around them.

suppose [səpóuz] v. (~이라고) 생각하다, 추측하다; 가정하다
If you suppose that something is true, you believe that it is probably true, because of other things that you know.

afraid [əfréid] a. 두려워하는, 겁내는; 걱정하는
If you are afraid of someone or afraid to do something, you are frightened because you think that something very unpleasant is going to happen to you.

shiver [ʃívər] v. (몸을) 떨다; n. 전율; 몸서리; 오한
When you shiver, your body shakes slightly because you are cold or frightened.

nod [nad] v. (고개를) 끄덕이다, 끄덕여 나타내다; n. (고개를) 끄덕임
If you nod, you move your head downward and upward to show agreement, understanding, or approval.

bother [báðər] v. 신경 쓰이게 하다, 괴롭히다; 귀찮게 하다; 신경 쓰다; n. 성가심
If something bothers you, or if you bother about it, it worries, annoys, or upsets you.

except [iksépt] prep. ~을 제외하고는, 외에는; v. 제외하다
You use except for to introduce the only thing or person that prevents a statement from being completely true.

wink [wiŋk] v. 윙크하다; (빛이) 깜박거리다; n. 윙크
When you wink at someone, you look toward them and close one eye very briefly, usually as a signal that something is a joke or a secret.

head [hed] v. (특정 방향으로) 향하다; ~을 이끌다; n. 머리, 고개; 책임자
If you are heading for a particular place, you are going toward that place.

stop short idiom 갑자기 멈추다, 중단시키다
If you stop short, you suddenly stop what you are doing.

bump [bʌmp] v. 부딪치다; 찧다; n. 쿵, 탁 (하고 단단한 것에 부딪치는 소리)
If you bump into something or someone, you accidentally hit them while you are moving.

exchange [ikstʃéindʒ] v. 교환하다, 주고받다; n. 교환; 대화
If two or more people exchange things of a particular kind, they give them to each other at the same time.

panic [pǽnik] n. 극심한 공포, 공황; v. 겁에 질려 어쩔 줄 모르다, 공황 상태에 빠지다 (panicky a. 당황한, 겁에 질린)
A panicky feeling or panicky behavior is characterized by panic.

blackboard [blǽkbɔ̀ːrd] n. 칠판
A blackboard is a dark-colored board that you can write on with chalk.

chart [tʃaːrt] n. 도표, 차트; v. 기록하다; 계획을 세우다
A chart is a diagram, picture, or graph which is intended to make information easier to understand.

graph [græf] n. 그래프, 도표
A graph is a mathematical diagram which shows the relationship between two or more sets of numbers or measurements.

conclude [kənklúːd] v. 끝내다, 마치다; 결론을 내리다
When you conclude, you say the last thing that you are going to say.

exaggerate [igzǽdʒərèit] v. 과장하다 (exaggeration n. 과장)
If you exaggerate, you indicate that something is, for example, worse or more important than it really is.

illuminate [ilúːmənèit] v. 분명히 하다; (불을) 비추다
(illuminating a. 이해를 돕는, 분명하게 하는)
If you illuminate something that is unclear or difficult to understand, you make it clearer by explaining it carefully or giving information about it.

shuffle [ʃʌfl] v. 발을 끌며 걷다; (발을) 이리저리 움직이다; n. 발을 끌며 걷기
If you shuffle somewhere, you walk there without lifting your feet properly off the ground.

clear one's throat idiom 헛기침을 하다
If you clear your throat, you cough once in order to make it easier to speak or to attract people's attention.

heroism [hérouìzm] n. 영웅적 행위, 용기 있는 행동
Heroism is great courage and bravery.

stuff [stʌf] n. 것(들), 물건; v. 채워 넣다; 쑤셔 넣다
You can use stuff to refer to things such as a substance, a collection of things, events, or ideas, or the contents of something in a general way without mentioning the thing itself by name.

stare [stɛər] v. 빤히 쳐다보다, 응시하다; n. 빤히 쳐다보기, 응시
If you stare at someone or something, you look at them for a long time.

go on idiom 말을 계속하다; (어떤 상황이) 계속되다; 시작하다
When you go on, you continue speaking after a short pause.

lock [lak] v. (자물쇠로) 잠그다; 고정시키다; n. 자물쇠 (lock in idiom ～을 가두다)
If you lock something or someone in a place, room, or container, you put them there and fasten the lock.

terrible [térəbl] a. 끔찍한, 소름 끼치는; 지독한
A terrible experience or situation is very serious or very unpleasant.

^{복습} **rescue** [réskjuː] v. 구하다, 구조하다, 구출하다; n. 구출, 구조; 구출 작업
If you rescue someone, you get them out of a dangerous or unpleasant situation.

^{복습} **exact** [igzǽkt] a. 정확한, 정밀한; 엄격한 (exactly ad. 맞아; 정확히, 틀림없이)
If you say 'Exactly,' you are agreeing with someone or emphasizing the truth of what they say.

^{복습} **resourceful** [risɔ́ːrsfəl] a. 임기응변의 재주가 있는, 재치 있는
Someone who is resourceful is good at finding ways of dealing with problems.

^{복습} **cheer** [ʧiər] v. 환호성을 지르다; 힘을 북돋우다; n. 환호(성)
When people cheer, they shout loudly to show their approval or to encourage someone who is doing something such as taking part in a game.

[*] **adventure** [ædvénʧər] n. 모험; 모험심
If someone has an adventure, they become involved in an unusual, exciting, and rather dangerous journey or series of events.

[*] **beam** [biːm] v. 활짝 웃다; 비추다; n. 빛줄기; 환한 미소
If you say that someone is beaming, you mean that they have a big smile on their face because they are happy, pleased, or proud about something.

[*] **assign** [əsáin] v. (일·책임 등을) 맡기다; 선임하다 (assignment n. 과제, 임무)
An assignment is a task or piece of work that you are given to do, especially as part of your job or studies.

^{복습} **whiz** [hwiz] v. 쌩 하고 움직이다; n. 윙 하는 소리
If something whizzes somewhere, it moves there very fast.

^{복습} **ride** [raid] v. (rode-ridden) (말·자전거·차량 등을) 타다;
n. (차량·자전거 등을) 타고 달리기; 여정
When you ride a bicycle or a motorcycle, you sit on it, control it, and travel along on it.

puddle [pʌdl] n. (빗물 등의) 물웅덩이

A puddle is a small, shallow pool of liquid that has spread on the ground.

splatter [splǽtər] v. (물·흙탕물 등을) 튀기다; 후두둑 떨어지다

If a thick wet substance splatters on something or is splattered on it, it drops or is thrown over it.

mud [mʌd] n. 진흙, 진창 (muddy a. 흙탕물의)

Something that is muddy contains mud or is covered in mud.

yell [jel] v. 소리치다, 외치다; n. 고함, 외침

If you yell, you shout loudly, usually because you are excited, angry, or in pain.

sigh [sai] v. 한숨을 쉬다, 한숨짓다; n. 한숨; 탄식

When you sigh, you let out a deep breath, as a way of expressing feelings such as disappointment, tiredness, or pleasure.

1장

page 5
아서와 버스터가 학교 계단을 올라가던 어느 아침, 그들 뒤에서 화난 목소리가 외쳤습니다. **"아서! 아서 리드!"**

아서가 몸을 돌렸습니다.

버스터도 함께 돌아보았습니다.

그 목소리는 프랜신의 것이었습니다. 그녀는 그들을 향해 급히 다가왔습니다. 머피와 수 엘렌이 그녀와 함께였습니다.

"무슨 일이야?" 아서가 물었습니다.

프랜신이 팔짱을 꼈습니다. "내가 무슨 일인지 말해줄게. 네가 모두에게 내가 마시멜로를 닮았다고 말했잖아."

page 6
"내가 그랬다고?"

버스터가 고개를 끄덕였습니다. "기억나지 않니, 아서? 그때 애가 그 바보 같은 스웨터를 입고 왔을 때 말이야. 여기저기 온통 부풀어 있던 그 옷 말이야."

"아, 그 스웨터." 아서는 이제 그것을 기억했습니다. 그 옷은 어깨에 패드가 들어가 있었고, 설탕 장식처럼 보풀이 일어나는 울 소재로 되어 있었습니다.

"너, 미안하다고 말하는 게 좋을 거야." 프랜신이 말했습니다.

"아니면 어쩔 건데?" 버스터가 말했습니다.

프랜신은 버스터를 무시했고 아서의 눈을 빤히 쳐다보았습니다.

"안 그랬다가는, 너는 똑똑히 당하게 될 거야."

"오, 그래?" 버스터가 말했습니다. "아서에게 그런 식으로 말하면 안 되지."

프랜신이 고개를 홱 치켜들었고 계속해서 계단을 올라갔습니다.

page 7
머피와 수 엘렌도 똑같이 했습니다.

"우리가 쟤들한테 잘 이야기한 것 같아." 버스터가 말했습니다.

"'우리'라고?" 아서가 말했습니다.

"나한테 고마워할 필요 없어." 버스터가 말하면서 아서의 어깨 위에 자기 팔을 둘렀습니다. "친구 좋다는 게 뭐니."

아서는 그저 한숨 쉬었습니다.

잠시 후, 그가 수업에 들어갔을 때, 그는 누군가가 자신을 노려보는 것을 느낄 수 있었습니다.

"이건 다 네 잘못이야." 그가 버스터에게 말했습니다.

버스터가 아서의 자리에 자기 몸을 밀어 넣었습니다. "내 잘못이라고?" 그가 말했습니다. "프랜신에게 마시멜로라고 말한 사람은 바로 너잖아."

"그리고 그렇게 거칠게 말한 사람은 바로 너잖아."

"난 그저 너의 편을 들어줬을 뿐이야."

"내가 혼자 힘으로 맞섰더라면 상황이 더 좋았을 거라고 생각해."

접힌 쪽지가 공중을 날아 아서의 책상 위에 떨어졌습니다. 그는 그 쪽지를 펼쳤고 조용히 소리 내어 읽었습니다.

page 9

"이건 네 마지막 경고야. 너는—"

버스터가 아서의 손에서 그 쪽지를 빼앗았습니다.

"... 아주 곤란하게 될 거야." 그가 계속 읽었습니다. "내 말은 아주 심각하게 말이야." 그가 잠시 멈추었습니다. "내 생각에 이건 해골 문양인 것 같아." 그는 생각하려고 말을 멈췄습니다. "이건 좋은 징조가 아니야."

아서가 몸을 돌려 프랜신을 보았습니다. 그녀는 여전히 그를 쏘아보고 있었습니다. 머피와 수 엘렌 역시 그를 노려보고 있었습니다.

"자, 주목하렴!" 랫번 선생님이 교실 앞에서 말했습니다. "버스터, 아마도 너는 네 자리로 돌아가는 것이 좋을 거야."

버스터는 아서의 의자에서 빠져나와 자기 자리로 재빠르게 돌아갔습니다.

"자." 랫번 선생님이 칠판 앞에 서서 말을 계속했습니다. "이제 수업을 시작하자. 여러분은 무엇이 남자 영웅 그리고 여자 영웅을 만드는지 궁금했던 적 있니? 그들은 태어날 때부터 용감하고 관대한 것일까, 아니면 나중에 그렇게 되는 것일까?"

page 10

아이들은 모두 서로를 쳐다보았습니다. 그들은 어리둥절했습니다. 그들이 질문에 대답해야 하는 것일까요, 아니면 랫번 선생님은 단지 혼잣말을 하는 것일까요? 그는 가끔 그러곤 했습니다.

"아무튼." 랫번 선생님이 계속 말했습니다. "이것이 바로 내가 주말 동안 너희가 생각해보길 바라는 거야."

모두 신음했습니다.

"여러분이 선택한 영웅에 대한 구두 보고서를 준비해야 한단다. 너희는 짝을 지어서 과제를 하게 될 거야." 랫번 선생님이 그의 메모를 살펴보았습니다. "빙키, 너는 수 엘런과 짝이란다. 머피, 너는 버스터와 함께 할 거야." 그는 몇몇 다른 짝들의 이름을 불렀습니다. "그리고 아서, 너는 프랜신과 한 팀이 될 거야."

아서는 프랜신을 힐끗 쳐다보았습니다. 그녀는 곧 죽을 것처럼 보였습니다.

그는 한숨을 쉬었습니다. 아주 긴 주말이 될 것 같았습니다.

2장

page 11

남자 영웅 그리고 여자 영웅. 그것이 바

로 아서와 버스터가 학교에서 집으로 돌아오는 길에 이야기를 나눈 주제였습니다.

"너는 누가 제일 좋아?" 버스터가 물었습니다. "그러니까, 우리가 선택할 수 있는 영웅은 많잖아. 우리가 현실 속의 영웅들을 조사하고 있다는 걸 알아. 하지만 로빈 후드나 헤라클래스는 어때?"

"아니면 바이오닉 버니도 있지." 아서가 말했습니다.

버스터가 고개를 끄덕였습니다. "그렇지." 그가 말했습니다.

page 12

아서는 그가 제일 좋아하는 영웅이 있는지 확신할 수 없었습니다. 그는 언제나 영웅들에 대한 이야기를 읽는 것을 좋아했지만, 무엇이 그들을 그들답게 만드는 것인지 혹은 그가 누구를 가장 좋아하는지에 대해서 생각했던 적이 없었습니다.

"내가 영웅들에 대해서 정말 좋아하는 점이 뭔지 알아?" 버스터가 말했습니다.

"뭔데?"

"음, 그들이 무척 영웅적이고, 정말 용감하다는 거야. 나는 그들이 하는 일들의 반만큼이라도 할 수 있으면 좋겠어."

"나도 그래." 아서가 말했습니다. 그는 잠시 말을 멈추었습니다. "넌 영웅들이 자기 친구를 마시멜로라고 부른 적이 있다고 생각하니?"

버스터는 확신할 수 없었습니다. "난 한 가지는 알아. 만약 그들이 그랬다 해도, 그들은 나중에 그것을 가지고 걱정하지는 않겠지."

아서는 고개를 끄덕였습니다. 만약 그가 조금 더 영웅적인 모습을 보일 수 있다면 분명히 이 상황에 도움이 될 것이었습니다.

아서가 집에 도착했을 때, 그는 D.W.가 부엌 전화로 통화하고 있는 것을 발견했습니다.

page 13

"그가 뭐라고 했다고?" D.W.가 헉 하고 숨을 쉬었습니다.

그녀는 잠시 동안 들었습니다.

"믿을 수 없어." 그녀가 계속 말했습니다. "뭐, 믿을 수도 있겠네. 아서가 저지르는 그 어떤 일도 나에게는 그다지 놀랍지 않아."

그녀가 자신의 오빠를 노려보았습니다.

아서는 자신의 고개를 저었습니다. 그는 요즘 노려보는 일을 많이 당했습니다.

"너 누구랑 말하는 거니?" 그가 물었습니다.

D.W.는 그를 무시했습니다. "으응...

글쎄, 오빠는 그런 말을 할 처지가 안 되지. 그가 잠옷을 입고 있을 때 어떻게 생겼는지 알아?... 아니... 아니야, 근데 그거 마음에 든다. 포기할래?"

"D.W.!" 아서가 소리쳤습니다.

"덤플링. 그는 질척거리는 덤플링처럼 보인다고."

아서가 전화기로 손을 뻗었습니다.

D.W.는 그를 막으려고 자신의 손을 들었습니다. "알았어." 그녀가 말했습니다. "내가 그에게 말할게. 안녕."

그녀는 전화를 끊었습니다.

page 15

"그거 나한테 온 것 아니야?" 아서가 말했습니다.

"맞기도 하고 아니기도 해." D.W.가 미소 지었습니다. "난 오빠에게 메시지를 전해줘야 해. 왜냐하면 프랜신이 오빠랑은 말하지 않겠다고 했거든."

"그녀가 그러지 않는다고?"

D.W.는 웃었습니다. "오빠는 누군가를 마시멜로라고 부르고 다니면서 그 사람이 신경 쓰지 않길 바랄 수는 없지."

"난 그게 그렇게 큰일인지 몰랐어." 아서가 말했습니다. "내 말은 그러니까, 나는 마시멜로를 좋아한단 말이야."

D.W.는 별로 감동 받지 않았습니다. "먹는 것으로는, 아마 그럴지도 몰라, 하지만 그렇게 보이고 싶지는 않을걸."

아서는 눈을 굴렸습니다. "그래서 메시지가 뭐야?" 그가 물었습니다.

"프랜신이 내일 3시에 도서관에서 자기와 만나자고 했어. 하지만 그녀가 오빠에게 말을 하지 않을 것이니까 오빠도 그녀에게 말을 걸면 안 돼."

아서가 한숨 쉬었습니다.

D.W.가 거들먹거렸습니다. "그리고 난 그녀를 탓하지 않아."

page 16

"그렇지만 우리가 말도 하지 않으면서 어떻게 무슨 일을 끝낼 수 있겠어?"

D.W.가 그를 향해 손가락을 까딱거렸습니다. "오빠는 사람들을 놀리기 전에 그 생각을 했어야지."

그 말을 끝으로, D.W.는 위층으로 올라가 버리면서, 만약 자신이 영웅이었다면 그가 이렇게 엉망인 상황에 빠지지 않았을 것이라고 생각하고 있는 아서를 뒤에 남겨 두었습니다.

3장

page 17

다음 날 오후, 아서가 엘우드시 도서관의 계단을 뛰어 올라가는 바로 그때 시계가 세 시를 알렸습니다.

휴우, 그가 생각했습니다.

그는 뒤뜰에서 팔과 함께 놀고 있었고, 시간 가는 것을 잊고 있었습니다.

그래서 그는 서둘러야만 했습니다. 만약 프랜신이 그를 기다려야 한다면, 그것은 그녀에게 또 다른 불평거리를 주게 될뿐입니다.

도서관 안에서, 아서는 도서관 사서 터너 선생님이 안내 데스크에 서 있는 것을 보았습니다. 프랜신이 그녀와 함께 있었습니다.

page 18

"터너 선생님, 안녕하세요." 그가 말했습니다.

사서는 그녀가 살펴보고 있던 책에서 고개를 들어 바라보았습니다. 그녀는 미소 지었습니다.

"안녕, 아서. 프랜신이 막 내게 너희의 보고서에 대해서 말해주고 있었단다."

아서는 지금쯤이면 프랜신이 그녀의 노려보는 시선을 다 써버렸길 바랐습니다. 그러나 그녀가 그를 향해 돌아보았을 때, 그는 그 시선이 여전히 강력하다는 것을 알 수 있었습니다.

"내가 말하고 있었던 대로." 프랜신이 말했습니다. "비록 우리가 이 보고서를 함께 수행하고 있지만, 내가 책임을 맡을 거야."

"오, 정말?" 아서가 말했습니다. "나는 랫번 선생님이 그런 말을 하신 것을 들은 기억은 없는데."

프랜신은 팔짱을 꼈습니다. "글쎄, 네가 그저 충분히 주의해서 듣지 않은 것이겠지. 아마 새로운 놀림거리를 생각하느라 너무 바빴나 보지."

"난 그러지 않았어!"

프랜신은 돌아섰습니다. "물론, 우리는 그것에 대해서 더 이야기하지 않을 텐데, 왜냐면 우리는 서로와 이야기하지 않기 때문이지."

page 20

"프랜신, 그것은 정말—"

"영웅은 많은 영감을 줄 수 있단다." 터너 선생님이 끼어들었습니다. "그렇게 생각하지 않니, 아서? 프랜신이 방금 자신의 생각들 중 몇 가지를 말해주었단다. 너는 어떤 종류의 영웅을 찾고 있니?"

"글쎄요." 아서가 말하면서, 자신을 진정시키려고 했습니다. "어디 보자. 당연히, 영웅적인 사람이어야겠죠."

"우와!" 프랜신이 말했습니다. "참 좋은 생각이야, 아서."

아서의 얼굴이 조금 빨개졌습니다. "나는 그저 소리 내서 생각하고 있는 것뿐이야. 그는 아마도—"

"여자는 어때?" 프랜신이 말했습니다.

"좋아." 아서가 말했습니다. "그녀가 무언가 유명한 일을 했다면 여자도 좋지."

page 21

터너 선생님은 카운터 위를 자신의

연필로 툭툭 쳤습니다. "잔 다르크는 어떠니?" 그녀가 말했습니다. "그녀는 확실히 유명하고, 또 역사상 가장 어린 지도자 가운데 한 사람이란다. 그녀는 영감을 주는 사람이고, 영국의 침략군들을 상대로 한 전투에서 프랑스 군대를 지휘했지. 그녀의 이야기에는 전투, 말─흥미진진한 것들이 있단다. 내가 생각하기에는 우리 도서관에 그녀에 대한 책이 유럽 역사 서가와 위인전 쪽에 있는 것 같구나."

"내가 위인전을 맡을래." 아서와 프랜신이 함께 말했습니다.

그들은 서로를 노려보았습니다.

"내가 먼저 말했어." 프랜신이 말했습니다.

"아니야!"

"맞아!"

"어머, 얘들아." 터너 선생님이 말했습니다. "이렇게 열정적인 모습을 보게 되어서 참 좋긴 하구나." 그녀는 그들의 찡그린 얼굴을 보았습니다. "하지만 아마 내가 결정하는 게 좋겠다. 프랜신, 네가 여기 먼저 왔으니까, 네가 위인전을 좀 살펴보지 그러니?"

"좋아요!" 프랜신이 말했습니다. 그녀가 아서에게 자신의 혀를 내밀었습니다.

page 22

"아서, 네 경우에는, 서고에 한번 가 보면 되겠다. 중세 프랑스 역사는 940번

서가에 있어. 그건 계단을 내려가서 모퉁이를 돌면 있단다."

아서가 고개를 끄덕였습니다.

프랜신은 복도를 따라서 걸어갔습니다.

"하지만 잊으면 안 된다." 터너 선생님이 그들의 뒤에서 외쳤습니다. "도서관 문은 닫을 거야, 정확히─"

"알고 있어요." 프랜신이 말했습니다. "5시 정각이에요."

4장

page 23

아서는 940.21번에서 프랑스 역사에 대한 큰 책을 찾았습니다. 아서는 터너 선생님이 아무것도 보지 않고도 그를 정확히 어디에 보내야 하는지 아는 것이 놀라웠습니다. 도서관 번호 시스템은 그를 헷갈리게 했습니다.

그 책은 표지에 유니콘과 긴 드레스를 입은 여자들로 꾸며진 태피스트리가 있었습니다. 책 속에서 아서는 많은 정보를 찾을 수 있었습니다. 몇몇 프랑스 사람들이 1066년에 영국을 정복했지만, 1400년대 초가 되자, 프랑스의 많은 지역이 영국 지배 아래 있었습니다.

page 24

그리고 프랑스 사람들은 그것을 좋아

하지 않았습니다.

두 손으로 책을 잡은 채, 아서는 대형 괘종시계 옆에 있는 크고, 안락한 소파 위로 자리를 잡았습니다. 그리고 그는 읽기 시작했습니다. 읽어야 할 일들이 아주 많았습니다. 오래 지나지 않아, 그의 눈꺼풀이 점점 무거워졌고, 그는 쿠션에 기대어 푹 쓰러져 버렸습니다.

"아서 경, 조심하시오!" 성첩에서 한 목소리가 외쳤습니다.

아서가 몸을 휙 숙이자 한 화살이 그의 머리 위로 아무것도 맞추지 못하고 쌩 하고 날아갔습니다.

"고맙소, 버스터 경!" 그가 외쳤습니다.

page 25

"프랑스 군이 그렇게 조준을 못하다니 우리가 운이 좋았소." 버스터 경이 말했습니다.

"정말이오." 아서 경이 말했습니다. "그렇지만 난 그들이 훈련을 많이 할 생각일까 봐 두렵소."

그가 있는 높은 위치에서, 아서는 전투지를 바라보았습니다. 프랑스군이 해자 너머에 엄청난 규모로 모여 있었습니다.

아서 경은 고개를 저었습니다. 이 모든 일은 단지 그가 프랑스 장군을 마시멜로라고 불렀기 때문에 일어났습니다.

그녀는 그것을 굉장히 불쾌하게 받아들였습니다.

그는 지금은 그 말을 후회하지만, 그렇다고 인정하기에 그는 자존심이 너무나 강했습니다. 게다가, 그 프랑스 장군은 사과를 받을 기분도 아닌 것처럼 보였습니다.

그녀는 자신의 군대 앞에서 자기 말을 타고 앞뒤로 왔다 갔다 하고 있었습니다.

"우리가 성을 차지할 것이다!" 그녀는 프랑스어로 말하고 있었습니다—그렇지만 어찌 된 일인지 아서는 그녀의 말을 이해할 수 있었습니다.

page 26

그녀의 군대가 환호했습니다.

"그러고 나면 우리는 여기서 누가 정말 마시멜로인지 확인할 것이다."

아서는 탑에 달린 시계가 종소리를 울리며 시간을 알리는 것을 들었습니다. 둥, 둥, 둥, 둥, 둥. 날이 저물고 있었습니다. 프랑스군은 여전히 공격할 계획일까요—아니면 아침까지 기다릴까요?

계단 위 모퉁이를 돈 곳에서 프랜신은 잔 다르크에 대한 챕터 북을 펼쳤습니다. 그곳은 아늑하고 조용히 있을 수 있었습니다. 그녀가 그 자리에 가만히 있는 한, 그녀는 아서를 마주칠 위험이 없었습니다. 프랜신은 책상다리를 하고 앉았고 그녀의 워크맨을 꽂았습니다. 그녀는 자신이 책을 읽는 동안에 들으려고 테이프를 가져왔습니다. 그렇게 한다면, 만약 아서가 그녀를 찾더라도, 그녀는 그를 손쉽게 모르는 척할 수 있을 것입니다.

page 28
책 자체는 매우 흥미로웠습니다. 그 책은 잔 다르크가 어떻게 프랑스 군대를 이끌고 오를레앙에서 영국군을 물리쳤는지에 대해 알려줬습니다. 그녀는 '오를레앙의 여자'라고 불렸습니다. 그녀가 싸우기 시작했을 때 그녀는 17살 정도밖에 되지 않았지만, 그녀는 갑옷을 입고 검을 들 수 있었습니다.

프랜신은 갑옷에 대해 궁금했습니다. 그것은 분명 무거웠을 것입니다. 만약 잔이 넘어진다면, 그녀는 일어나는 데 도움이 필요했을까요?

음악을 따라 흥얼거리면서, 그녀가 계속 읽어나가는 동안 복도 끝 창문에서 빛이 점점 사라지고 있었습니다.

5장

page 29
아서는 하품을 했습니다. 그는 잠을 자려던 것이 아니었습니다. 그저 낮잠이 그에게 살며시 다가왔습니다. 그는 게으르게 기지개를 켰습니다. 그는 도서관이 잠을 자기에 좋은 곳이라고 생각해 본 적이 없었지만, 그곳은 확실히 조용했습니다.

그는 일어나서 메인 데스크 쪽으로 걸어서 돌아갔습니다. 그가 들을 수 있는 유일한 소리는 자기 발걸음 소리뿐이었습니다. 그것은 조금 이상한 것 같았습니다. 물론, 도서관은 조용해야 하지만, 이건 너무 조용한 것 같았습니다.

"터너 선생님?" 아서가 불렀습니다.

아무도 대답하지 않았습니다.

page 30
아서가 주변을 둘러보았습니다. 많은 전등이 꺼져 있었습니다. 그것 또한 이상했습니다. 그는 정문으로 달려가서 손잡이를 당겼습니다.

문은 잠겨 있었습니다! 아서는 그가 할 수 있는 한 가장 세게 손잡이를 흔들었습니다.

문은 여전히 잠겨 있었습니다.

갑자기 괘종시계가 울리기 시작했습니다.

둥, 둥, 둥, 둥, 둥, 둥!

아서는 세고 있었습니다. 6번의 둥! 그것은 6시를 의미했습니다. 하지만 도서관은 5시에 닫습니다. 그는 터너 선생님이 그 사실을 말했던 것을 확실하게 기억했습니다. 그것은 도서관이... 닫혔다는 것을 의미했습니다!

아서는 무서웠습니다. 어떻게 도서관이 닫힐 수가 있지? 그는 여전히 안에 있는데 말입니다. 도서관은 안에 사람이 있는 채로 닫혀서는 안 됐습니다.

아서는 침을 꿀꺽 삼켰습니다. 만약 그가 다른 사람 없이 자신만 이 안에 있는 것이라면, 그것은 그가 혼자라는 뜻이었습니다. 정말 혼자 말입니다.

page 32

갑자기 도서관의 익숙한 구석구석이 그다지 친숙하게 보이지 않았습니다. 바닥을 가로질러 움직이는 저 그림자들이 그를 잡으려 하는 건 아닐까요? 아니, 아니요, 그것들은 그저 바람에 날리는 나뭇가지들의 그림자들일 뿐입니다. 그렇지만 책들은 어떤가요? 만약 그가 그것들을 등지고 돌아서면, 그것들이 선반에서 날아와 그의 등을 때리는 것은 아닐까요?

아서는 자신의 두 눈을 질끈 감았습니다. 침착해, 그는 자신에게 말했습니다. 이건 그저 도서관일 뿐이야.

그는 다시 한 번 살펴보기 위해 한쪽 눈을 떴습니다. 모두 정상처럼 보였습니다. 그는 다른 쪽 눈도 떴습니다. 그림자는 자신들의 일에만 몰두하고 있었습니다. 책들은 서고에서 움직이지도 않았습니다.

우당탕!

아서가 번쩍 뛰었습니다. 그 소리는 그의 상상이 아니었습니다. 그의 상상은 저런 소음을 만들 수 없었습니다.

아서는 입술을 깨물었습니다. 아마도 그는 도서관에 혼자 있는 것이 아닌가 봅니다. 그 생각은 그의 기분을 좋게 만들어야 했지만—실은 그렇지 않았습니다.

page 33

"저기요? 거기 누구 있나요?"

아무도 대답하지 않았습니다. 아서는 주변을 돌아보며, 걸어갔습니다. 누군가 혹은 무엇이 그 요란한 소리를 만들었습니다. 그는 더 찾아보아야 했습니다.

그의 가슴 속에 심장이 쿵쾅거리며 뛰는 채로, 그는 앞으로 몇 걸음 더 내디뎠습니다. 그는 조용히 걸으려고 노력했지만, 그의 운동화 밑에서 바닥이 삐걱거렸습니다.

그가 계단에 이르렀을 때, 아서는 계단을 위아래로 보았습니다. 두 방향 모두 어둡고 무서워 보였습니다.

이러한 상황에서 잔 다르크라면 어떻게 했을까? 아서는 궁금했습니다. 그녀는 적어도 전투를 위해서 무장한 상태였을 것입니다. 아서가 자신을 보호하기 위해 가진 유일한 것은 연필뿐이었습니다—그리고 그것마저도 깎을 필요가 있었습니다.

page 34

아서는 주의 깊게 들었습니다. 더 요

란한 소리가 나지 않았습니다. 아마 첫 번째 것은 우연히 책더미가 떨어졌던 것일 겁니다. 아마도 그는 조금 긴장을 풀고—도서관을 빠져나가는 데에만 집중하면 될 것입니다.

그리고 그때 어떤 손이 뒤에서 그의 어깨를 잡았습니다.

6장

page 35

"아아악!" 아서가 소리 질렀습니다. 그가 몸을 휙 돌렸습니다.

"아아악!" 프랜신도 같이 소리 질렀습니다. 그녀는 그의 바로 뒤에 서 있었습니다.

그들 두 사람은 잠시 동안 몸을 떨면서, 그냥 그곳에 서 있었습니다.

"너 왜 소리 지른 거야?" 그녀가 소리쳤습니다.

"너도 소리 질렀잖아." 아서가 말했습니다.

"네가 먼저 소리 질렀으니까 그렇지."

아서는 깊은숨을 들이마셨습니다. "글쎄, 왜 내가 소리를 지르면 안 되니? 나는 어두운 도서관에 혼자 있잖아. 나는 요란한 소리도 들었는데—"

"그건 요란한 소리가 아니었어." 프랜신이 말했습니다. "내가 우연히 책상에서 책 몇 권을 건드려 떨어트렸어. 거의 아무 소리도 나지 않았다고."

page 36

"나한테는 요란한 소리로 들렸어." 아서가 주장했습니다. "그리고 나는 살펴보기 위해 갔고, 이 소름 끼치는 손이 내 어깨를 잡은 거야—"

"내 손은 소름 끼치지 않아." 프랜신이 말했습니다. "아주 예쁜 손이지." 그녀가 그것을 바라보았고 미소 지었습니다. 그리고 그녀의 미소는 인상으로 바뀌었습니다. "그나저나, 너 여기서 뭐 하는 거니?"

아서가 자신의 허리에 손을 짚었습니다. "그 질문은 내가 너한테 해야 할 것 같은데." 그가 말했습니다.

프랜신은 한숨 쉬었습니다. "나는 터너 선생님을 찾고 있었어. 그러다가 나는 시계가 울리는 것을 들었지. 6시가 지났어, 너도 알다시피."

"나도 숫자를 셀 줄 알아, 프랜신."

프랜신은 아랑곳하지 않았습니다. "그러시겠지. 그런데 너 한 시간 전에는 어디 있던 거니?"

"책을 좀 보고 있었지."

"그럼, 왜 나를 찾으러 오지 않았니? 도서관 문이 닫히고 있었잖아. 5시에, 기억나? 네가 우리를 갇히게 한 거야."

page 38

아서의 얼굴이 빨개졌습니다. "그렇지

않아!"

"그럼 무슨 일이 있었던 건데?"

아서는 망설였습니다. "그게, 사실, 난 잠들었어."

"잠이 들었다고!" 프랜신이 웃었습니다. "너 되게 바보 같다고 느끼겠다."

아서는 얼굴을 찌푸렸습니다. "아마 그럴 수도 있고, 아닐 수도 있지. 그렇지만 적어도 난 변명거리는 있잖아. 너는 어떻고? 네가 그렇게 시간을 잘 기억했으면서, 왜 넌 *나*를 찾으러 오지 않은 거야?"

이제 프랜신의 얼굴이 빨개질 차례였습니다.

"알았어, 알았어, 나는 책을 살펴보는 동안 음악을 듣고 있었어. 나도 시계를 듣지 못한 것 같아."

"하! 그럼 네가 나보다 더 신경을 쓰고 있던 것도 아니네."

"관두자." 프랜신이 말했습니다. "나는 너랑 다투고 있을 시간이 없어. 나는 이곳에서 빠져나가야만 해."

"좋아," 아서가 말했습니다. "너는 계획이 있니?"

"계획?"

"여기서 빠져나갈 방법 말이야." 아서가 찡그렸습니다. "네가 말한 대로, 우리는 갇혔잖아."

"한 가지 생각하고 있어." 그녀가 콧방귀를 뀌었습니다. "그리고 그게 준비가 되면, 나는 그걸 실행에 옮길 거야. 그렇지만 나는 네게 내 생각을 말해주지 않을 거야. 왜 그런 줄 아니? 왜냐면 나는 여전히 너랑 말하지 않고 있거든. 또, 나는 듣고 있지도 않고 말이야."

그녀의 뜻을 완전히 명확하게 하려고, 프랜신은 자신의 귀에 자기 손가락을 꽂고 걸어가 버렸습니다.

7장

page40

비록 아서와 프랜신이 함께 궁리하고 있지는 않았지만, 그들 둘 다 다음에 무엇을 할지에 대해 같은 생각을 했습니다.

아마 나는 창문을 넘어서 밖으로 나갈 수 있을 거야, 아서가 생각했습니다.

나는 창문을 시도해 봐야겠어, 프랜신이 생각했습니다.

아서는 곧 무너질 듯한 책더미를 쌓기 시작했습니다. 그가 다 했을 때, 그는 타고 올라가기 시작했습니다.

그 책더미는 앞뒤로 흔들렸습니다.

아서가 막 창문 손잡이를 잡으려고 했을 때 프랜신이 다가왔습니다. 아서의 책더미에 있는 책 한 권이 자신의 예쁘고, 깔끔한 책더미를 완성시키는 데 딱 알맞은 크기였습니다.

page 41

그녀가 책을 홱 잡아당겼습니다.

아서의 책더미가 쓰러졌습니다. 아서는 쿵 소리를 크게 내며 바닥에 부딪쳤습니다.

"너 더 조심해서 물건을 쌓아야겠다." 프랜신이 말했습니다.

마지막 책이 제자리에 놓이자, 프랜신의 책더미는 완벽하게 안정적이었습니다. 그녀는 창문을 향해서 올라갔고 걸쇠를 당겼습니다.

그것은 움직이지 않았습니다.

그녀는 몇 번 더 세게 당겼지만, 걸쇠는 움직이지 않았습니다.

파리가 그녀의 얼굴 앞에서 윙윙거렸습니다.

"저리 가!" 프랜신이 말했습니다. "네가 알아서 나갈 방법을 찾으란 말이야."

그녀가 파리를 향해 손을 세차게 흔들었습니다.

"후아아아!" 프랜신이 굉음을 내며 땅에 떨어졌습니다.

아서는 모퉁이를 돌아 달려오다 바닥에 누워 있던 프랜신에게 걸려 넘어질 뻔했습니다.

page 43

"무슨 일이야?" 그가 물었습니다.

프랜신이 자신의 몸을 일으켜 세웠습니다. "내가 균형을 잃었어." 그녀가 그에게 말을 하지 않기로 한 것을 잊고 말

했습니다.

"창문은 어떻게 됐어?"

프랜신은 고개를 저었습니다. "잊어버려." 그녀가 말했습니다. "내 생각엔 이 창문들은 오랫동안 열린 적이 없는 것 같아."

"이런!"

"뭐야?" 프랜신이 톡 쏘아붙였습니다.

"나 방금 무언가를 기억했어." 아서가 말했습니다. "오늘은 토요일이잖아. 그렇다면 도서관은 닫혀 있을 텐데—"

"월요일까지!" 프랜신이 그를 대신해서 말을 끝맺었습니다. 그녀는 침을 꿀꺽 삼켰습니다. "저 소음은 뭐지?"

"어떤 소음?"

"나 우르릉거리는 소리가 들려."

아서가 내려다보았습니다. "내 배에서 나는 거야. 그게 주말 내내 음식을 못 먹는다는 생각을 하고 있나 봐."

"우리는 네 배보다 걱정해야 할 것이 더 많아."라고 프랜신이 말했습니다. "우리 가족들은 몹시 걱정할 거야."

page 44

아서는 D.W.가 이 소식을 어떻게 받아들일지 생각해 보았습니다. 그는 그녀가 그의 포스터들을 떼어 버리고, 그의 장난감을 다 던져 버리고, 벽을 핑크색으로 칠하는 모습을 머릿속에 그릴 수 있었습니다.

"모두는 아닐 걸." 그가 말했습니다.

"잠깐만!" 프랜신이 말했습니다. "나 알아냈어."

그녀는 카드 목록으로 달려갔고 목록들을 휙휙 넘겨보기 시작했습니다.

"너 미쳤니?" 아서가 말했습니다. "어떻게 책이 우리를 도와줄 수 있겠어?"

프랜신은 그를 무시했습니다. "어디 보자." 그녀가 말했습니다. "'감옥에서 탈출하는 방법', '무인도에서 탈출하는 방법'... 아하!"

"아하, 뭔데?" 아서가 말했습니다.

"'도서관에서 탈출하는 방법'이지, 당연히."

아서는 감명받았습니다. 그는 이런 종류의 일이 그렇게 자주 일어날 것이라고 깨닫지 못했습니다.

"이봐! 나랑 같이 가!" 그가 말하면서, 서고 쪽으로 프랜신을 뒤따라갔습니다.

page 45

그녀는 책이 있는 자리를 찾았습니다. 이것은 이 하나가 빠진 뒤 짓는 미소 속 틈처럼 구멍이 나 있었습니다.

"난 믿을 수가 없어! 이미 도서관 안에 있지 않은 한, 누가 도서관에서 탈출하는 방법에 대한 책을 필요로 하겠어? 그리고 만약 누군가 우리와 여기 함께 있다면"—그녀는 주변을 둘러보았습니다—"우리가 알았을 텐데."

"그래서, 이젠 어쩌지?" 아서가 말했다.

프랜신이 한숨 쉬었습니다. "나도 그걸 알면 좋겠어."

8장

page 46

전에도 도서관은 어두워 보였습니다. 지금은 어쩐지 훨씬 더 어둡게 보였습니다. 방들은 전에도 조용한 것 같았습니다. 이제 방들은 거의 침묵 속에 얼어붙은 것 같았습니다.

따리링!

"저건 뭐지?" 프랜신이 물었습니다. 그녀가 아서를 쳐다보았습니다.

"전화야!" 그들이 동시에 말했습니다.

그들은 메인 데스크로 정신없이 뛰어갔습니다. 전화는 여전히 울리고 있었습니다.

프랜신이 수화기를 잡아들었습니다. "여보세요?"

page 47

"터너 선생님, 안녕하세요." 전화상의 목소리가 말했습니다. "저 머피 크로스와이어예요. 저에게 아직 기회가 없었는데—"

"머피!" 프랜신이 말을 자르고 끼어들었습니다. "나야, 프랜신. 저기 들어봐,

나 갔었는데—"

"아, 미안해, 프랜신, 내가 실수로 너에게 걸었나 봐. 나는 도서관에 전화하려고 한 건데. 이런, 지금 통화할 수 없겠네. 저녁 식사를 알리는 종소리가 들리거든. 다음에 또 이야기해. 안녕."

그녀가 전화를 끊었습니다.

"머피! 잠깐만! 머피?" 프랜신이 전화기를 쳐다보았습니다.

"너 뭐 한 거니?" 아서가 소리쳤습니다. "어떻게 그녀의 전화를 끊을 수가 있어?"

"내가 그녀 전화를 끊은 게 아니야. 그녀가 내 전화를 끊은 거야. 어쨌든, 나는 우리 엄마한테 전화할 거니까, 조금 진정해."

프랜신이 자신의 집 번호로 전화를 걸었습니다. 그녀는 삑 소리와 함께 녹음된 내용을 들었습니다.

"죄송합니다. 도서관 밖으로 전화를 걸기 위해서는 반드시 올바른 사용자 번호를 입력해야 합니다. 끊고 다시 시도해 주세요."

"사용자 번호라고?" 프랜신이 전화기를 쳐다보았습니다. "하지만 나는 사용자 번호를 모르는걸."

그녀는 어쨌든 다시 걸어 보았습니다.

"죄송합니다. 도서관 밖으로 전화를 걸기 위해서는 반드시—"

프랜신은 전화기를 쾅 하고 내려놓았습니다. "사용자 번호! 비밀번호! 이 세상이 어떻게 돌아가는 거야, 도대체?"

"우리는 망했어." 아서가 말했습니다.

"오, 아서, 좀 진정해. 넌 정말 겁쟁이야."

"내가? 글쎄, 너는 권위적이고, 전부 다 아는 체하는... 마쉬멜로야."

"더 이상은 못 참아, 아서 리드! 만약 내가 여기서 주말을 보내야 한다면, 나는 너랑 같이 보내진 않을 거야!"

그녀는 쿵쾅대며 방 밖으로 뛰쳐나갔습니다.

"난 상관없어." 아서가 그녀 뒤에 대고 소리쳤습니다. 그는 점점 우울해져 가는 주위를 둘러보았습니다. "내가 어디 신경이나 쓰는지 봐." 그가 조용히 덧붙였습니다.

혼자 남겨진 채, 아서는 뭐 할 것이 없나 주변을 둘러보았습니다. 그는 잡지 한 권을 들고 휙휙 넘겨보기 시작했습니다. 어느 한 장에 구운 칠면조 사진이 있었습니다.

아서의 배가 꼬르륵거렸습니다.

"저거 정말 맛있어 보인다." 그가 중얼거렸습니다. 그는 그 책장의 일부를 찢었고 그것을 씹어보려고 했습니다.

"윽!" 그가 뱉으면서, 말했습니다. 그것은 전혀 칠면조 맛이 나지 않았습니다.

쿵!

저건 뭐지?

쿵!

아서는 얼굴을 찡그렸습니다. 도서관에서는 저런 쿵쾅거리는 소음이 나지 말아야 했습니다.

"프랜신?"

그녀는 대답하지 않았습니다.

아서는 다시 잡지로 돌아왔습니다. 그는 매시 포테이토와 그레이비가 칠면조 다리보다 더 맛있을지 궁금했습니다.

page 50

쿵!

아서는 잡지를 내려놓았습니다.

"프랜신!" 그가 불렀습니다.

그 이름이 복도 사이로 울려 퍼졌습니다.

그녀는 어디에 있는 거지? 아서는 프랜신이 갔던 방향으로 움직이기 시작했습니다.

"프랜신! 프랜신! 너 어디 있니?"

쿵!

또 그 소리가 들렸습니다. 그리고 이번에 그는 여자아이의 비명도 들었습니다.

"프랜신! 걱정하지 마! 내가 가고 있어."

아서는 계단을 뛰어 올라가 위층으로 갔습니다. 그는 자신이 도착한 첫 번째 문을 열었습니다.

그곳은 빗자루 벽장이었습니다.

아서는 계속 갔습니다. 그는 복도 끝에 있는 또 다른 문에서 더 많은 비명이 나는 것을 들었습니다.

아서는 문을 향해 급히 달려갔습니다. 그는 그 반대편에서 사악한 웃음소리가 나는 것을 들었습니다.

page 52

그는 낭비할 시간이 없었습니다. 프랜신이 곤경에 빠졌습니다! 그는 숨을 깊게 들이마셨고─불쑥 들어갔습니다.

9장

page 53

방에 들어가면서 아서는 카펫에 걸려 바닥에 넘어졌습니다. 그의 안경이 휙 벗겨졌고 방을 가로질러 날아갔습니다.

그것은 피자 상자 가운데에 떨어졌습니다.

아서는 눈을 가늘게 뜨고 주변을 둘러보았습니다.

"프랜신, 너 괜찮니?"

프랜신은 의자에 앉아서 TV를 보고 있었습니다.

"물론 괜찮지. 내가 왜 괜찮지 않겠어?"

아서는 바닥을 재빨리 가로질렀고 자

신의 안경을 집어 들었습니다. 치즈 가닥이 렌즈에 매달려 있었습니다.

page 54

아서는 그것을 닦아내고 다시 안경을 썼습니다.

"난 확신하지 못했어." 그가 말했습니다. "난 쿵쾅거리는 소리를 들었다고."

"아, 그거 말이야... 내가 보고 있는 영화에 큰 발을 가진 괴물이 나와."

"그리고 비명도!"

"당연하지. 이건 공포 영화인걸."

"그리고 사악한 웃음도." 아서가 계속 말했습니다.

"알아." 프랜신이 말했습니다. "그 괴물이 특이한 유머 감각이 있거든."

"너도 마찬가지야!" 아서가 말했습니다. "네가 대답하지 않았을 때, 난 네가 다치거나 어떻게 된 줄 알았어. 나는 걱정했단 말이야. 난 너를 구해주러 왔다고." 그가 둘러보았습니다. "그나저나, 우리 어디에 있는 거야?"

프랜신은 어깨를 으쓱했습니다. "여긴 직원 사무실인 것 같아, 내 생각엔. 나는 도서관 사서들이 이렇게 잘 먹는지 몰랐어. 난 냉장고에서 피자를 찾았고 그것을 전자레인지에 돌려서 데웠어."

"프랜신, 우리 확실히 짚고 넘어가자. 우리는 도서관에 갇혔어. 날은 점점 어두워지고 있어. 우리는 여기에 얼마나 오래 갇혀 있어야 하는지도 몰라. 그런데 너는 여기 앉아서 피자를 먹고 텔레비전을 보고 있었니?

page 55

그녀가 고개를 끄덕였습니다. "넌 틀림없이 내가 얼마나 임기응변이 좋은지 정말 몰랐을걸."

그것은 사실이었지만, 아서는 그것을 인정하려 하지 않았습니다. "글쎄, 난 딱 한 가지 말할 것이 있어."

"그리고 그게 뭔데?"

아서의 배가 꼬르륵거렸습니다. "너는 나누어 먹을 생각이 있니?"

프랜신은 그것을 생각해 보았습니다. "내가 왜 나를 마시멜로라고 부르는 사람과 같이 나누어 먹어야 하니?"

"누가 할 소리인데. 너 기억력이 좋지 않구나. 내가 안경을 샀을 때 기억나? 너 그때 나를 안경잡이라고 불렀잖아."

"글쎄, 나는... 그건 정말 오래 전 일이야." 그녀가 잠시 말을 멈췄습니다. "저기, 너 나를 구해주러 왔다고 말했니?"

"그런 셈이지."

page 56

"그랬잖아, 그렇지?" 프랜신이 또 다른 접시를 들어 올렸습니다. "너 정말 용감했어, 아서. 잔 다르크도 기뻤을 거야." 그녀는 잠시 말을 멈췄습니다. "피자 좀 먹을래?"

"물론이지."

잠시 후, 아서와 프래신은 자신들의 의자에 편하게 앉았습니다.

"으어어어!" 아서가 신음을 냈습니다.

"두 배로 으어어어!" 프랜신이 말했습니다.

피자는 없어졌고, 칩과 쿠키가 들어 있던 빈 봉지 몇 개가 주위에 흩어져 있었습니다.

아서가 미소 지었습니다. "이건 내가 생각했던 것보다 더 좋은데. 심부름도 없고, 숙제도 없고, 또 없는 건... D.W.!"

그는 깜짝 놀라서 똑바로 앉았습니다. 그의 여동생 D.W.가 갑자기 문가에 나타났습니다.

"안녕, 아서." 그녀가 말했습니다. "오빠는 *커다란* 곤경에 처했어."

바로 그때, 아서의 아버지와 프래신의 어머니가 모퉁이를 돌아왔습니다. 터너 선생님이 그들과 함께 있었습니다.

page 58

"아서! 프랜신!" 리드 씨가 말했습니다.

"너희 모두 괜찮다니 정말 다행이야!" 프렌스키 부인이 말했습니다.

터너 선생님이 고개를 저었습니다. "나는 어떻게 이런 일이 일어났는지 정말 모르겠구나. 하지만 너희 둘 다 보게 되어서 정말 기쁘구나."

"너희 모두 괜찮니?" 리드 씨가 물었습니다.

"다치진 않았니?" 프렌스키 부인이 물었습니다.

D.W.가 칩, 쿠키, 그리고 빈 피자 상자를 한번 둘러보았습니다.

"걱정하지 마세요." 그녀가 말했습니다. "제 생각에는 그들은 살아남을 것 같으니까요."

10장

page 59

월요일 아침 학교에서는, 모두 이야기 전체를 들으려고 주변에 모여 있었습니다.

"난 늘 생각했었어." 빙키가 말했습니다. "도서관이 문을 닫고 나면 책 속의 등장인물들이 놀러 나온다고 말이야. 난 너희가 그런 것을 본 것 같진 않은데."

"물론 아니지." 프랜신이 말했습니다. "그들은 유령을 무서워하거든."

"유령이라고!" 버스터가 말했습니다. 그는 조금 몸을 떨었습니다.

프랜신이 고개를 끄덕였습니다. "그렇지만 그 애들은 우리를 괴롭히지는 않았어."

"그 머리 없던 유령 빼고는 말이지." 아서가 말했습니다. "그렇지, 프랜신?"

그들은 서로에게 윙크했습니다.

page 60
종이 울리자, 아이들은 그들의 교실로 향했습니다.

"그래서, 너는 누구에 대해서 보고서를 썼니?" 버스터가 아서에게 물었습니다.

아서는 갑자기 멈춰 섰습니다. 프랜신이 그와 부딪칠 뻔했지만, 그녀 역시, 갑자기 멈췄습니다.

"보고서?"

아서와 프랜신은 당황한 표정을 주고받았습니다. 그 모든 소동으로, 그들은 잔 다르크에 대해서 잊고 말았던 것입니다.

그 표정이 여전히 그들의 얼굴에 남아있는 동안 머피가 잠시 후 그녀의 보고서를 마무리 지었습니다. 칠판에는 크로스와이어 모터스 차트와 그래프가 나란히 세워져 있었습니다.

"그래서." 그녀가 끝을 맺었습니다. "에드워드 크로스와이어가 없었다면 지금 우리가 아는 엘우드시는 없었을 거라고 말하는 것도 과장은 아닙니다."

"정말, 음, 계몽적이구나, 머피." 랫번 선생님이 말했습니다. "그다음으로."—그는 자신의 메모를 내려다보았습니다—"아서와 프랜신."

page 61
두 파트너는 느릿느릿 교실 앞으로 걸어갔습니다. 그들은 학급 앞에 서서 목을 가다듬었습니다.

"음." 아서가 말했습니다. "우리는 우리 보고서 주제로 잔 다르크를 골랐습니다. 그렇지만 우리는 우리가 할 수 있는 만큼 많이 배울 기회를 갖지는 못했는데요..."

"왜냐하면." 프랜신이 갑자기 말했습니다. "우리는 영웅적 행동에 대한 진정한 의미를 배우느라 무척 바빴기 때문입니다. 그것은 단지 책에서 찾을 수 있는 것이 아닙니다. 그것은 현실이에요."

아서가 그녀를 빤히 쳐다보았습니다.

"그래요." 프랜신이 계속 말했습니다. "우리가 도서관에 갇혀 있었을 때, 그건 정말 끔찍할 수 있었습니다. 사실, 그건 처음에는 끔찍했는데, 왜냐하면 우리가 싸우고 그랬기 때문이에요. 그때 아서가 제가 위험에 빠진 줄 알고 저를 구하러 왔습니다."

"맞아요." 아서가 말했습니다. "그리고 프랜신도 또한, 정말 용감했고 재치가 있었어요. 그녀는 음식이 어디에 있는지 찾아냈죠. 그리고 저를 주려고 피자를 남겨 두었습니다."

page 62
반 친구들이 환호했습니다.

"그것 정말 좋구나." 랫번 선생님이 말했습니다. "너희의 모험이 너희에게 중요한 무언가를 가르쳐준 것 같구나."

아서와 프랜신은 서로를 보며 활짝 웃

었습니다.

"그래서 내가 너희에게 과제를 할 수 있게 내일까지 시간을 주도록 하지."

"우리가 그 모든 걸 겪었는데도 불구하고요?"라고 프랜신이 말했습니다.

"응 그래," 랫번 선생님이 말했습니다. "그건 너희 보고서에 특별한 의미를 부여할 거야."

그날 늦게, 아서와 버스터가 학교에서 집으로 걸어가고 있었습니다.

"난 이 말을 하기 싫지만." 버스터가 말했습니다. "프랜신은 그렇게 나쁘진 않아."

아서가 고개를 끄덕였습니다. "그녀는 정말 재미있을 수 있어. 그녀는 좋은 친구야."

page 64

그 순간, 프랜신이 자신의 자전거를 타고 쌩 하고 지나갔습니다. 그녀는 물웅덩이 위로 곧장 내달리면서, 소년들에게 흙탕물을 튀겼습니다.

"미안해애애애!" 그녀가 자신의 어깨 너머로 소리쳤습니다.

아서와 버스터는 자신들의 젖은 셔츠를 내려다보았습니다.

아서가 한숨 쉬었습니다. "하지만 그 누구도 완벽하진 않지." 그가 말했습니다.

Chapter 1

1. D "What's up?" asked Arthur. Francine folded her arms. "I'll tell you what's up. You told everyone I looked like a marshmallow."

2. B Buster nodded. "Don't you remember, Arthur? She was wearing that goofy sweater, the one that puffs up everywhere." "Oh, *that* sweater." Arthur remembered it now. It had padded shoulders and wool that fluffed out like frosting.

3. A "This is all your fault," he said to Buster. Buster wedged himself into Arthur's seat. "*My* fault?" he said. "You're the one who called Francine a marshmallow." "And you're the one who talked so tough."

4. C "*This is your final warning. You are—*" Buster grabbed the note out of Arthur's hand. "*. . . in big trouble,*" he continued. "*And I mean BIG.*" He paused. "I think that's a skull and crossbones." He stopped to think. "That's not a good sign."

5. A "Please prepare an oral report on the hero or heroine of your choice. You'll be working in pairs." Mr. Ratburn consulted his notes. "Binky, you're with Sue Ellen. Muffy, you'll be working with Buster." He named some other pairs. "And Arthur, you're teamed with Francine."

Chapter 2

1. A Heroes and heroines. That's what Arthur and Buster talked about on their way home from school. "Who's your favorite?" Buster asked. "I mean, there are a lot of heroes to choose from. I know we're studying the ones from real life. But what about Robin Hood or Hercules?" "Or the Bionic Bunny," said Arthur.

2. B She hung up the phone. "Wasn't that for me?" said Arthur. "Yes and no." D.W. smiled. "I have to give you the message because Francine isn't talking to you."

3. C D.W. ignored him. "Uh-huh . . . Well, he should talk. Guess what he looks like in his pajamas? . . . No . . . No, but I like that one. Give up?" "D.W.!" Arthur shouted. "A dumpling. He looks like a soggy dumpling."

4. C "Yes and no." D.W. smiled. "I have to give you the message because Francine isn't talking to you." "She's not?" D.W. laughed. "You can't go around calling someone a marshmallow and expect her not to care."

5. B Arthur rolled his eyes. "So what was the message?" he asked. "Francine says to meet her at the library tomorrow at three. But you can't speak to her because she's not speaking to you."

Chapter 3

1. B He had been playing in the backyard with Pal and had lost track of the time. So he had needed to hurry. If Francine had to wait for him, that would just give her something else to complain about.

2. C If Francine had to wait for him, that would just give her something else to complain about.

3. A Ms. Turner tapped her pencil on the counter. "How about Joan of Arc?" she said. "She was certainly famous, and one of the youngest leaders in history. She was an inspiration, leading the French army in battle against the English invaders. Her story has battles, horses—exciting stuff. I believe we have books about her in the European History section as well as in the biographies."

4. B "Goodness, children," said Ms. Turner. "It's nice to see such enthusiasm." She looked at their frowning faces. "But maybe I should decide. Francine, you were here first, so why don't you look in the biographies."

5. D "But don't forget," Ms. Turner called after them, "the library will close promptly at—" "We know," said Francine. "Five o'clock."

Chapter 4

1. C Arthur found a big book on French history at 940.21. He was impressed that Ms. Turner knew just where to send him without looking anything up. The library number system was confusing to him.

2. A The book had a tapestry on the front, decorated with unicorns and women in long dresses. Inside, Arthur found a lot of information. Some of the

French had conquered England in 1066, but by the early 1400s, much of France was under English control.

3. B *Sir Arthur shook his head. All this had happened just because he had called the French general a marshmallow. She had taken great offense at that.*

4. B Up the stairs and around the corner, Francine had opened a chapter book about Joan of Arc.

5. D Francine sat down cross-legged and put on her Walkman. She had brought a tape to play while she read. That way, even if Arthur found her, she could easily ignore him.

Chapter 5

1. A He stood up and walked back toward the main desk. The only sound he heard was his own footsteps. That seemed odd. The library was supposed to be quiet, of course, but this seemed *too quiet.* "Ms. Turner?" Arthur called out. Nobody answered. Arthur looked around. A lot of the lights were off. That was odd, too. He ran to the front door and pulled the handle. The door was locked! Arthur shook it as hard as he could. The door stayed locked. Suddenly the grandfather clock began to chime. *Bong, bong, bong, bong, bong, bong!*

2. D Arthur was scared. How could the library be closed? He was still inside it. Libraries weren't supposed to close with people inside them.

3. B *Crassshhh!* Arthur jumped. That sound was not his imagination. His imagination couldn't make up a noise like that. Arthur bit his lip. Maybe he wasn't alone in the library. The thought should have made him feel better—but it didn't.

4. D When he reached the stairs, Arthur looked up and down the stairwell. Both directions looked dark and scary. What would Joan of Arc have done in this situation? Arthur wondered. She at least would have been armed for battle. The only thing Arthur had to protect himself with was a pencil—and even that needed sharpening. Arthur listened carefully. There had been no further crashes.

5. A Maybe he could relax a little—and concentrate on getting out of the library. And then a hand grabbed his shoulder from behind.

Chapter 6

1. D "Why did you scream?" she cried. "You screamed, too," said Arthur. "Only because you screamed first."

2. B Arthur took a deep breath. "Well, why shouldn't I scream? I'm alone in a dark library. I hear a crash—" "That wasn't a crash," said Francine. "I accidentally knocked some books off a desk. It barely made any noise at all."

3. A She was not impressed. "So you say. But where were you an hour ago?" "Looking through some books." "Well, why didn't you come find me? The library was closing. Five o'clock, remember? You got us locked in."

4. C Now it was Francine's turn to blush. "Okay, okay, I was listening to music while I looked through the books. I guess I didn't hear the clock, either."

5. D "I'm working on one," she sniffed. "And when it's ready, I'll put it into operation. But I'm not going to share my ideas with you. Do you know why? Because I'm still not talking to you. And I'm not listening, either."

Chapter 7

1. B Even though Arthur and Francine were not working together, they both had the same idea about what to do next. Maybe I can climb out a window, thought Arthur. I think I'll try the window, thought Francine.

2. C She gave it a few tugs, but the latch didn't move. A fly buzzed in front of her face. "Go away!" said Francine. "Find your own way out." She waved her hand wildly at the fly. "Whoaaaa!" Francine landed with a crash.

3. D "I hear growling." Arthur looked down. "That's my stomach. It's thinking about getting no food for the entire weekend."

4. B Francine ignored him. "Let's see," she said. *"How to Escape from Prison, How to Escape from a Desert Island* . . . Aha!" "Aha, what?" said Arthur. *"How to Escape from a Library,* of course."

5. C She found the place for the book. It made a hole like the gap in a smile after a tooth has fallen out. "I don't believe it! Who would need a book on escaping from a library unless they were already *in* a library? And if someone was here with us"—she looked around—"I guess we would know about it."

Chapter 8

1. D *"Hello, Ms. Turner,"* said the voice on the line. *"This is Muffy Crosswire. I didn't get a chance to*—" "Muffy!" Francine cut in. "It's me, Francine. Listen, I'm locked—"

2. B Francine dialed her home number. She heard a beep and then a recording. *"We're sorry. To dial out of the library, you must enter the correct user code. Please hang up and try again."* "User code?" Francine stared at the phone. "But I don't know the user code."

3. D Left to himself, Arthur looked around for something to do. He picked up a magazine and started flipping through it. There was a picture of a roast turkey on one page. Arthur's stomach grumbled. "That sure looks good," he muttered. He ripped off part of the page and tried chewing it.

4. C "Francine! Francine! Where are you?" *Thump!* There it was again. And this time he also heard a girl screaming. "Francine! Don't worry! I'm coming."

5. B Arthur ran up the steps to the next level. He threw open the first door he came to. It was a broom closet.

Chapter 9

1. D As he entered the room, Arthur tripped on the rug and fell to the floor. His glasses flew off and sailed across the room. They landed in the middle of a pizza box.

2. C "I wasn't sure," he said. "I heard thumping." "Oh, that . . . The movie I'm watching has monsters with big feet." "And screaming!" "Naturally. It's a horror movie." "And evil laughing," Arthur went on. "I know," said Francine. "The monsters have a strange sense of humor."

3. B "So do you!" said Arthur. "When you didn't answer, I figured you were hurt or something. I was worried. I was coming to your rescue." He looked around. "Where are we, anyway?" Francine shrugged. "It's the staff room, I think. I had no idea librarians were so well fed. I found the pizza in the refrigerator and zapped it in the microwave."

4. D "Well, I . . . That's ancient history." She paused. "Hey, did you say you were coming to my rescue?" "Sort of." "You were, weren't you?" Francine picked up another plate. "That was very brave of you, Arthur. Joan of Arc would be pleased." She paused. "Want some pizza?"

5. A He sat up in horror. His sister D.W. had suddenly appeared in the doorway. "Hello, Arthur," she said. "You're in *big* trouble." Just then, Arthur's father and Francine's mother came around the corner. Ms. Turner was with them.

Chapter 10

1. C Monday morning at school, everyone was crowding around to hear the full story.

2. B "I've always thought," said Binky, "that the characters in books come out to play after the library closes. I don't suppose you saw any."

3. A "Report?" Arthur and Francine exchanged a panicky look. In all the excitement, they had forgotten about Joan of Arc.

4. D "That's very good," said Mr. Ratburn. "It looks like your adventure taught you something important." Arthur and Francine beamed at each other. "So I'll give you until tomorrow to do your assignment." "After all we've been through?" said Francine. "Oh, yes," said Mr. Ratburn. "It should give your report special meaning."

5. A Later that day, Arthur and Buster were walking home from school. "I hate to say it," said Buster, "but Francine's not so bad." Arthur nodded. "She can be a lot of fun. She's a good friend." At that moment, Francine whizzed by on her bike. She rode right through a puddle, splattering the boys with muddy water.

아서, 도서관에 갇히다!
(Arthur Locked in the Library!)

1판 1쇄   2015년 10월 12일
1판 5쇄   2020년 8월 7일

지은이   Marc Brown
기획   이수영
책임편집   정소이 김보경
콘텐츠제작및감수   롱테일북스 편집부
저작권   김보경
마케팅   김보미 정경훈

펴낸이   이수영
펴낸곳   (주)롱테일북스
출판등록   제2015-000191호
주소   04043 서울특별시 마포구 양화로 12길 16-9(서교동) 북앤빌딩 3층
전자메일   helper@longtailbooks.co.kr
(학원 · 학교에서 본도서를 교재로 사용하길 원하시는 경우 전자메일로 문의주시면
자세한 안내를 받으실 수 있습니다.)

ISBN 979-11-86701-02-7 14740

롱테일북스는 (주)북하우스 퍼블리셔스의 계열사입니다.

이 도서의 국립중앙도서관 출판시도서목록(CIP)은 서지정보유통지원시스템 홈페이지(http://seoji.nl.go.kr)와
국가자료공동목록시스템(http://www.nl.go.kr/kolisnet)에서 이용하실 수 있습니다. (CIP 제어번호 : CIP 2015024029)

Arthur
Locked in the Library!

ISBN 979-11-86701-02-7 14740

Longtail Books

For the Quadri crew:

Colleen, Hayley, and Shea

Chapter 1

Arthur and Buster were walking up the school steps one morning when an angry voice shouted behind them, "ARTHUR! ARTHUR READ!"

Arthur turned.

Buster turned, too.

The voice **belong**ed to Francine. She was **charging** toward them. Muffy and Sue Ellen were with her.

"What's up?" asked Arthur.

Francine **fold**ed her arms. "I'll tell you what's up. You told everyone I looked like a marshmallow.★"

"I did?"

Buster **nod**ded. "Don't you remember, Arthur? She was wearing that **goofy** sweater, the one that **puffs up** everywhere."

"Oh, *that* sweater." Arthur remembered it now. It had **pad**ded shoulders and wool that **fluff**ed out like frosting.✶

"You'd better say you're sorry," said Francine.

"Or what?" said Buster.

Francine **ignore**d Buster and **stare**d Arthur in the eye.

"**Or else** you're going to **get it**."

"Oh, yeah?" said Buster. "You can't talk to Arthur that way."

Francine **toss**ed her head and continued up the steps.

★ **marshmallow** 마시멜로. 젤라틴과 달걀 흰자, 설탕, 향료, 식용색소 등을 섞어 만든 쫄깃쫄깃한 과자.

✶ **frosting** 프로스팅. 설탕으로 만든 혼합물로 케이크나 쿠키를 장식하는 데 사용한다.

Muffy and Sue Ellen did the same.

"I guess we told *them*," said Buster.

"'We'?" said Arthur.

"You don't have to thank me," said Buster, putting his arm around Arthur's shoulders. "That's what friends are for."

Arthur just **sigh**ed.

A little while later, when he went into class, he could feel himself being **glare**d at.

"This is all your **fault**," he said to Buster.

Buster **wedge**d himself into Arthur's seat. "*My* fault?" he said. "You're the one who called Francine a marshmallow."

"And you're the one who talked so **tough**."

"I was just **stand**ing **up for** you."

"I think it might be better if I stood up for myself."

A folded note flew through the air and **land**ed on Arthur's desk. He unfolded it and read it aloud quietly.

7

*"This is your final **warning**. You are—"*

Buster **grab**bed the note out of Arthur's hand.

". . . in big trouble," he continued. *"And I mean BIG."* He **pause**d. "I think that's a skull and crossbones.★" He stopped to think. "That's not a good **sign**."

Arthur turned around and looked at Francine. She was still glaring at him. Muffy and Sue Ellen were glaring at him, too.

"**Attention**, please!" said the teacher, Mr. Ratburn, from the front of the room. "Buster, perhaps you would **consider** taking your own seat."

Buster pulled himself out of Arthur's chair and **zip**ped back to his own.

"Now," Mr. Ratburn continued, standing at the **blackboard**, "let's get started. Have you ever **wonder**ed what makes a hero or heroine?

★ **skull and crossbones** 해골 밑에 대퇴골 두 개를 엇갈리게 배치한 그림으로 해적선 깃발·독극물 용기 등에 위험 경고의 표시로 쓰인다.

9

Are people born brave and **generous,** or do they become this way later on?"

The kids all looked at one another. They were **puzzled. Were** they **supposed to** answer the question, or was Mr. Ratburn just talking to himself? He did that sometimes.

"Anyway," Mr. Ratburn **went on,** "that's what I want you to think about this weekend."

Everyone **groan**ed.

"Please **prepare** an **oral** report on the hero or heroine of your choice. You'll be working in **pairs.**" Mr. Ratburn **consult**ed his notes. "Binky, you're with Sue Ellen. Muffy, you'll be working with Buster." He named some other pairs. "And Arthur, you're teamed with Francine."

Arthur **glance**d at Francine. She looked like she was going to die.

He sighed. It was going to be a very long weekend.

Chapter
2

Heroes and heroines. That's what Arthur and Buster talked about on their way home from school.

"Who's your **favorite**?" Buster asked. "I mean, there are a lot of heroes to choose from. I know we're studying the ones from real life. But what about Robin Hood★ or Hercules?✳"

"Or the Bionic Bunny," said Arthur.

Buster **nod**ded. "**Exact**ly," he said.

★ **Robin Hood** 로빈 후드. 중세 영국의 전설적인 영웅이자 의적.
✳ **Hercules** 헤라클레스. 그리스 신화 속 가장 힘이 세고 유명한 영웅으로 제우스와 알크메네의 아들이다.

Arthur wasn't sure he had a favorite. He had always liked reading stories about heroes, but he had never thought much about what made them the way they were or which ones he liked best.

"You know what I really like about heroes?" said Buster.

"What?"

"Well, that they're so **heroic**, so brave. I wish I could do half the things they do."

"Me, too," said Arthur. He **paused**. "Do you think heroes ever call their friends marshmallows?"

Buster wasn't sure. "I know one thing. If they do, they don't worry about it later."

Arthur nodded. It would **certain**ly help things if he could be a little more heroic himself.

When Arthur got home, he found D.W. talking on the kitchen phone.

"He said *what?*" D.W. **gasp**ed.

She listened for a moment.

"I can't believe it," she **went on**. "Well, I **suppose** I can. Nothing Arthur does really surprises me."

She **glare**d at her brother.

Arthur shook his head. He was being glared at a lot **lately**.

"Who are you talking to?" he asked.

D.W. **ignore**d him. "Uh-huh . . . Well, he should talk. Guess what he looks like in his **pajamas**? . . . No . . . No, but I like that one. **Give up**?"

"D.W.!" Arthur shouted.

"A dumpling.* He looks like a **soggy** dumpling."

Arthur **reach**ed for the phone.

D.W. held up her hand to stop him. "Okay," she said. "I'll tell him. Bye."

She **hung up** the phone.

★ **dumpling** 밀가루와 계란을 끓는 스프나 스튜에 넣어서 익히는 요리.

"Wasn't that for me?" said Arthur.

"Yes and no." D.W. smiled. "I have to give you the message because Francine isn't talking to you."

"She's not?"

D.W. laughed. "You can't **go around** calling someone a marshmallow and **expect** her not to care."

"I didn't know it was such a **big deal**," said Arthur. "I mean, I like marshmallows."

D.W. was not **impress**ed. "To eat, maybe, but not to look like."

Arthur **roll**ed **his eyes**. "So what was the message?" he asked.

"Francine says to meet her at the library tomorrow at three. But you can't speak to her because she's not speaking to you."

Arthur **sigh**ed.

D.W. **stuck her nose in the air.** "And I don't **blame** her."

"But how **are** we **supposed to** get any work done if we're not speaking?"

D.W. **wag**ged her finger at him. "You should have thought of that before you started **call**ing people **names**."

And with that, D.W. went upstairs, leaving Arthur thinking that if he were a hero, he wouldn't be in this **mess**.

Chapter 3

The next afternoon, Arthur ran up the steps of the Elwood City library just as the clock **struck** three.

Phew, he thought.

He had been playing in the **backyard** with Pal and had **lost track of** the time. So he had needed to hurry. If Francine had to wait for him, that would just give her something else to **complain** about.

Inside the library, Arthur saw the **librarian**, Ms. Turner, standing by the **reference** desk. Francine was with her.

"Hello, Ms. Turner," he said.

The librarian looked up from the book she was **consult**ing. She smiled.

"Good afternoon, Arthur. Francine was just telling me about your report."

Arthur had hoped that Francine might have **use**d **up** her **glare** by now. But as she turned toward him, he could see that it was still going strong.

"As I was saying," said Francine, "even though we're **work**ing **on** this report together, I'm in **charge**."

"Oh, really?" said Arthur. "I don't remember Mr. Ratburn saying anything about that."

Francine **fold**ed her arms. "Well, you just weren't listening closely enough. Probably too busy **think**ing **up** new **insults**."

"I was not!"

Francine turned away. "Of course, we're not going to **discuss** it **further**, because we're not

speaking to each other."

"Francine, that's the most—"

"Heroes can be so **inspirational**," Ms. Turner **put in**. "Don't you agree, Arthur? Francine was just telling me some of her ideas. What **sort** of hero are you looking for?"

"Well," said Arthur, trying to **get** himself **under control**. "Let's see. Someone **heroic**, of course."

"Ooooh!" said Francine. "Good thought, Arthur."

Arthur **turn**ed a little **red**. "I'm just **think**ing **out loud**. He might be—"

"What about a *she?*" said Francine.

"Okay," said Arthur. "A woman is fine as long as she did something famous."

Ms. Turner **tap**ped her pencil on the **counter**. "How about Joan of Arc?*" she said. "She was

---

★ **Joan of Arc** 잔 다르크(Jeanne d'Arc). 프랑스와 영국의 백년전쟁에서 '프랑스를 구하라'는 신의 계시를 받고 전투에 나가 나라를 위기에서 구한 영웅적인 소녀.

certainly famous, and one of the youngest **lead**ers in **history**. She was an **inspiration**, leading the French **army** in **battle** against the English **invade**rs. Her story has battles, horses—exciting **stuff**. I believe we have books about her in the European History **section** as well as in the **biographies**."

"I'll take biographies," Arthur and Francine said together.

They **stare**d at each other.

"I called it first!" said Francine.

"You did not!"

"Did, too!"

"**Goodness**, children," said Ms. Turner. "It's nice to see such **enthusiasm**." She looked at their **frown**ing faces. "But maybe I should decide. Francine, you were here first, so why don't you look in the biographies."

"Yes!" said Francine. She **stuck out** her **tongue** at Arthur.

"As for you, Arthur, you could try the **stack**s.

Medieval French history is in the 940s. That's down the stairs and around the corner."

Arthur nodded.

Francine **head**ed down the **aisle**.

"But don't forget," Ms. Turner called after them, "the library will close **prompt**ly at—"

"We know," said Francine. "Five o'clock."

Chapter

4

Arthur found a big book on French **history**
at 940.21. He was **impress**ed that Ms. Turner
knew just where to send him without looking
anything up. The library number system★ was
confusing to him.

The book had a tapestry✳ on the front,
decorated with unicorns❋ and women in long
dresses. Inside, Arthur found a lot of information.

★ **library number system** 도서관 분류번호. 멜빌 듀이가 만든 듀이 십진분류
법(DDC)에 따른 것으로 900번대에는 역사서가 분류되어 있다.

✳ **tapestry** 태피스트리. 색색의 실로 그림이나 무늬를 짜 넣은 벽걸이 또는 실내
장식용 직물.

❋ **unicorn** 유니콘. 이마에 뿔이 한 개 나 있는 말의 모습을 한 신화 속 동물.

Some of the French had **conquer**ed England in 1066, but by the early 1400s, much of France was under English control.

And the French didn't like that.

Holding the book in both hands, Arthur **settle**d onto a big, **comfortable** couch next to a grandfather clock.★ Then he started to read. There were tons of facts to **get through**. Before long, his **eyelid**s grew heavy, and he **slump**ed down against the cushion.

*"**Look out**, Sir Arthur!" cried a voice from the battlement.*✶

*Arthur **ducked** as an **arrow whizzed harmlessly** over his head.*

"Thank you, Lord✳ *Buster!" he called out.*

★ **grandfather clock** 대형 괘종시계. 추에 의해 움직이는 진자가 몸체 속에 들어 있는 시계. 시계의 몸체가 크고 바닥에 꼿꼿하게 바로 서 있다.

✶ **battlement** 성첩. 성벽 위에 덧쌓은 낮은 담. 전투시 병사들은 이곳에 몸을 숨기고 활을 쏘거나 다른 무기를 사용하여 적을 격퇴하였다.

✳ **Lord** 경(卿). 영국에서 귀족의 작위를 받은 사람을 높여 이르는 말.

"We are lucky the French have such poor **aim**," said Lord Buster.

"True," said Sir Arthur. "But I fear they plan to do a lot of **practicing**."

From his **perch**, Arthur looked out over the field of **battle**. The French **army** had **gather**ed in great **force** outside the **moat**.

Sir Arthur shook his head. All this had happened just because he had called the French general* a marshmallow. She had **taken** great **offense at** that.

He **regret**ted the comment now, but he was too **proud** to **admit** it. Besides, the French general didn't seem in the **mood** for **apologies**.

She was **riding** her horse **back and forth** in front of her **troop**s.

"We will take the castle!" she was saying in French—although Arthur could **somehow** understand

---

★ general 군대의 계급인 장군.

25

her.

*Her army **cheer**ed.*

"Then we will see who is the marshmallow around here."

*Arthur heard the clock in the tower ringing out the hour. **Bong**, bong, bong, bong, bong. The day was growing late. Did the French still plan to attack—or would they wait until morning?*

Up the stairs and around the corner, Francine had opened a chapter book about Joan of Arc. It was nice and **private** here. As long as she **stay**ed **put**, she wouldn't have to **risk run**ning **into** Arthur.

Francine sat down **cross-legged** and put on her Walkman.★ She had brought a tape to play while she read. That way, even if Arthur found her, she could **easily ignore** him.

★**Walkman** 워크맨. 개인 휴대용 카세트 테이프 플레이어.

The book itself was pretty interesting. It told of how Joan of Arc **led** the French army and **defeat**ed the English at Orléans. The **Maid** of Orléans,★ she was called. She was only about seventeen when she started fighting, but she got to wear **armor** and carry a **sword**.

Francine **wonder**ed about the armor. It must have been heavy. If Joan ever fell down, did she need help getting up?

Humming to the music, she kept reading as the light **fade**d in the windows at the end of the **aisle**.

★ **Maid of Orléans** 오를레앙의 여자. 잔 다르크의 별명으로 그녀가 오를레앙 전투에 참가하여 큰 승리를 거두었기에 이와 같이 불리게 되었다.

Chapter

5

Arthur **yawn**ed. He hadn't meant to fall asleep. The **nap** had just **sneak**ed **up** on him. He **stretch**ed lazily. He had never thought of the library as a good place to sleep, but it **certain**ly was quiet.

He stood up and walked back toward the main desk. The only sound he heard was his own **footstep**s. That seemed **odd**. The library **was supposed to** be quiet, of course, but this seemed *too quiet*.

"Ms. Turner?" Arthur called out.

Nobody answered.

Arthur looked around. A lot of the lights were off. That was odd, too. He ran to the front door and pulled the **handle**.

The door was **lock**ed! Arthur shook it as hard as he could.

The door stayed locked.

Suddenly the grandfather clock began to **chime**.

Bong, bong, bong, bong, bong, bong!

Arthur was **count**ing. Six bongs! That meant six o'clock. But the library closed at five. He **distinct**ly remembered Ms. Turner **mention**ing that fact. That meant the library was . . . closed!

Arthur was **scare**d. How could the library be closed? He was still inside it. Libraries weren't supposed to close with people inside them.

Arthur **gulp**ed. If he was inside by himself, that meant he was alone. Very alone.

Suddenly the library's **familiar nook**s and

crannies didn't look so friendly. Were those shadows moving across the floor to **grab** him? No, no, they were just the shadows of **branches blow**n by the wind. What about the books, though? If he **turn**ed **his back on** them, would they fly off the **shelves** and hit him in the back?

Arthur **squeeze**d his eyes shut. Stay **calm**, he told himself. It's only a library.

He opened one eye to take another look. Everything seemed normal. He opened the other. The shadows were **mind**ing **their own business**. The books hadn't moved from the **stack**s.

Crassshhh!

Arthur jumped. That sound was not his **imagination**. His imagination couldn't **make up** a noise like that.

Arthur **bit** his lip. Maybe he wasn't alone in the library. The thought should have made him feel better—but it didn't.

"Hello? Is anyone there?"

No one answered. Arthur walked along, looking around. Someone or something had made that crash. He had to find out more.

With his heart **pound**ing in his **chest**, he took a few steps forward. He tried to walk silently, but the floor **creak**ed under his **sneaker**s.

When he **reach**ed the stairs, Arthur looked up and down the stairwell.* Both directions looked dark and **scary**.

What would Joan of Arc have done in this situation? Arthur wondered. She at least would have been **arm**ed for **battle**. The only thing Arthur had to protect himself with was a pencil—and even that needed **sharpen**ing.

Arthur listened carefully. There had been no **further** crashes. Maybe the first one was

---

★ stairwell 계단통. 건물 내부에 계단이 나 있는 공간.

a **fluke**, a **pile** of books that had fallen over. Maybe he could **relax** a little—and **concentrate** on getting out of the library.

And then a hand grabbed his shoulder from behind.

Chapter
6

"Aagghh!" Arthur screamed. He **whirl**ed around.

"Aagghh!" Francine screamed back. She was standing right behind him.

The two of them just stood there, shaking for a moment.

"Why did you scream?" she cried.

"You screamed, too," said Arthur.

"Only because you screamed first."

Arthur took a deep **breath**. "Well, why shouldn't I scream? I'm alone in a dark library. I hear a **crash**—"

"That wasn't a crash," said Francine. "I

accidentally knocked some books off a desk. It barely made any noise at all."

"It sounded like a crash to me," Arthur insisted. "And then I go to investigate, and this creepy hand grabs me on the shoulder—"

"My hand isn't creepy," said Francine. "It's a very nice hand." She looked at it and smiled. Then her smile turned to a frown. "Anyway, what are you doing here?"

Arthur put his hands on his hips. "I could ask you the same question," he said.

Francine sighed. "I was looking for Ms. Turner. Then I heard the clock chiming. It's after six, you know."

"I can count, Francine."

She was not impressed. "So you say. But where were you an hour ago?"

"Looking through some books."

"Well, why didn't you come find me? The library was closing. Five o'clock, remember?

You got us **lock**ed in."

Arthur **blush**ed. "I did not!"

"So then what happened?"

Arthur **hesitated**. "Well, actually, I fell asleep."

"Asleep!" Francine laughed. "You must feel pretty **silly**."

Arthur **made a face**. "Maybe I do, and maybe I don't. But at least I have an **excuse**. What about you? Since you remember the time so well, why didn't you come find *me*?"

Now it was Francine's turn to blush. "Okay, okay, I was listening to music while I looked through the books. I guess I didn't hear the clock, either."

"Ha! So you weren't paying any more **attention** than I was."

"**Never mind** that," said Francine. "I don't have time to **argue** with you. I have to get out of here."

"Fine," said Arthur. "Do you have a plan?"

"A plan?"

"A way to get out." Arthur frowned. "As you said, we're locked in."

"I'm **work**ing **on** one," she **sniff**ed. "And when it's ready, I'll **put** it **into operation**. But I'm not going to share my ideas with you. Do you know why? Because I'm still not talking to you. And I'm not listening, either."

To **make the point** perfectly clear, Francine **stuck** her fingers in her ears and walked away.

Chapter 7

Even though Arthur and Francine were not working together, they both had the same idea about what to do next.

Maybe I can climb out a window, thought Arthur.

I think I'll try the window, thought Francine.

Arthur began **piling** up a **rickety** pile of books. When he was done, he began climbing up.

The pile **sway**ed **back and forth**.

Arthur **was about to grab** the window **handle** when Francine **came by**. One of the books in Arthur's pile was **exact**ly the size she needed to complete a nice, **neat** pile of her own.

She **yank**ed out the book.

Arthur's pile fell down. Arthur hit the floor with a loud **thud**.

"You should build things more carefully," said Francine.

With the last book **in place**, Francine's pile was perfectly **steady**. She climbed up to the window and **gave** the **latch a pull**.

It was **stuck**.

She gave it a few **tug**s, but the latch didn't move.

A fly **buzz**ed in front of her face.

"Go away!" said Francine. "Find your own way out."

She **wave**d her hand wildly at the fly.

"Whoaaaa!" Francine **land**ed with a **crash**.

Arthur came running around the corner and almost **trip**ped over Francine, who was lying on the floor.

"What happened?" he asked.

Francine **pick**ed **herself up**. "I lost my **balance**," she said, forgetting that she wasn't talking to him.

"What about the window?"

Francine shook her head. "**Forget it**," she said. "I don't think these windows have been opened in a long time."

"Uh-oh!"

"What?" Francine **snap**ped.

"I just remembered something," said Arthur. "Today is Saturday. That means the library is closed until—"

"Monday!" Francine finished for him. She **gulp**ed. "What's that noise?"

"What noise?"

"I hear **growl**ing."

Arthur looked down. "That's my **stomach**. It's thinking about getting no food for the entire weekend."

"We have more than your stomach to worry

about," said Francine. "Our families will be worried sick."

Arthur thought about how D.W. would take the news. He could picture her pulling down his **posters, throw**ing **out** his toys, and painting the walls pink.

"Not everyone," he said.

"Wait a minute!" said Francine. "I've got it."

She ran to the card **catalog** and began **flip**ping **through** the **listing**s.

"Are you crazy?" said Arthur. "How is a *book* going to help us?"

Francine **ignore**d him. "Let's see," she said. *"How to Escape from **Prison**, How to Escape from a **Desert Island** . . .* Aha!"

"Aha, what?" said Arthur.

"How to Escape from a Library, of course."

Arthur was **impress**ed. He hadn't **realize**d that this **sort** of thing happened so often.

"Hey! Wait for me!" he said, following Francine

into the **stack**s.

She found the place for the book. It made a hole like the **gap** in a smile after a tooth has fallen out.

"I don't believe it! Who would need a book on escaping from a library unless they were already *in* a library? And if someone was here with us"—she looked around—"I guess we would know about it."

"So, now what?" said Arthur.

Francine sighed. "I wish I knew."

Chapter

8

The library had seemed dark before. Now **somehow** it seemed even darker. The rooms had seemed silent before. Now they seemed almost **frozen** in quiet.

Rinnggg!

"What's that?" asked Francine. She looked at Arthur.

"PHONE!" they said together.

They **race**d back to the main desk. The phone was still ringing.

Francine **grab**bed the **receiver**.

"Hello?"

"Hello, Ms. Turner," said the voice **on the line**. *"This is Muffy Crosswire. I didn't get a chance to—"*

"Muffy!" Francine **cut in**. "It's me, Francine. Listen, I'm **lock**ed—"

*"Oh, sorry, Francine, I must have **dial**ed you by mistake. I meant to call the library. Ooops, can't talk now. I hear the bell for dinner. I'll talk to you later. Bye."*

She **hung up**.

"Muffy! Wait! Muffy?" Francine **stare**d at the phone.

"What did you do?" Arthur shouted. "How could you hang up on her?"

"I didn't hang up on her. She hung up on me. Anyway, I'm calling my mother, so **relax**."

Francine dialed her home number. She heard a *beep* and then a **recording**.

*"We're sorry. To dial out of the library, you must enter the correct user **code**. Please hang up and try again."*

"User code?" Francine stared at the phone. "But I don't know the user code."

She tried again anyway.

"We're sorry. To dial out of the library, you must enter—"

Francine **slam**med down the phone. "User codes! Passwords! What's this world **coming to**, anyway?"

"We're **doom**ed," said Arthur.

"Oh, Arthur, just relax. You're such a **wimp**."

"Me? Well, you're a **bossy, know-it-all** . . . marshmallow."

"**That does it**, Arthur Read! If I have to spend the weekend here, I'm not spending it with you!"

She **storm**ed out of the room.

"Fine with me," Arthur called after her. He looked around at the **deepen**ing **gloom**. "See if I care," he added softly.

Left to himself, Arthur looked around for

something to do. He picked up a magazine and started **flip**ping **through** it. There was a picture of a **roast turkey** on one page.

Arthur's **stomach grumble**d.

"That sure looks good," he **mutter**ed. He **rip**ped off part of the page and tried **chew**ing it.

"**Yuck!**" he said, **spit**ting it out. It didn't taste like turkey at all.

Thump!

What was that?

Thump!

Arthur **frown**ed. Libraries **were** not **supposed to** make thumping noises.

"Francine?"

She didn't answer.

Arthur went back to the magazine. He **wonder**ed if the **mash**ed potatoes★ and gravy※ would taste

---

★ mashed potato 삶은 감자를 으깬 뒤 버터와 우유를 섞어서 만드는 요리.

※ gravy 그레이비. 고기를 익힐 때 나온 육즙에 와인, 밀가루 등을 넣어서 만든 소스.

any better than the turkey leg.

Thump!

Arthur put down the magazine.

"Francine!" he called out.

The name **echo**ed through the **hall**s.

Where was she? Arthur started moving in the direction that Francine had gone.

"Francine! Francine! Where are you?"

Thump!

There it was again. And this time he also heard a girl screaming.

"Francine! Don't worry! I'm coming."

Arthur ran up the steps to the next level. He threw open the first door he came to.

It was a **broom closet**.

Arthur kept going. He heard more screaming coming from another door down the hall.

Arthur raced toward the door. He heard **evil laughter** coming from the other side.

There was no time to **waste**. Francine was

in trouble! He took a deep **breath**—and **burst** in.

Chapter 9

As he entered the room, Arthur **trip**ped on the **rug** and fell to the floor. His glasses flew off and **sail**ed across the room.

They **land**ed in the middle of a pizza box.

Arthur **squint**ed and looked around.

"Francine, are you okay?"

Francine was sitting in a chair watching television.

"Of course I'm okay. Why wouldn't I be?"

Arthur **scrambled** across the floor and picked up his glasses. **Strand**s of cheese **dangle**d from the **lens**es.

Arthur **wipe**d them off and put the glasses back on.

"I wasn't sure," he said. "I heard **thump**ing."

"Oh, that . . . The movie I'm watching has **monster**s with big feet."

"And screaming!"

"Naturally. It's a **horror** movie."

"And **evil** laughing," Arthur **went on**.

"I know," said Francine. "The monsters have a **strange** sense of **humor**."

"So do you!" said Arthur. "When you didn't answer, I **figure**d you were hurt or something. I was worried. I was coming to your **rescue**." He looked around. "Where are we, anyway?"

Francine **shrug**ged. "It's the **staff** room, I think. I had no idea **librarian**s were so well **fed**. I found the pizza in the **refrigerator** and **zap**ped it in the **microwave**."

"Francine, let me **get** this **straight**. We're locked in the library. It's getting dark. We don't know how long we're going to be **stuck** here. And you're sitting here eating pizza and watching TV?"

She **nod**ded. "I'll **bet** you had no idea I could be so **resourceful**."

That was true, but Arthur **wasn't about to admit** it. "Well, I only have one thing to say."

"And what's that?"

Arthur's **stomach grumbled**. "Were you planning to share?"

Francine **considered** it. "Why should I share with someone who calls me a marshmallow?"

"Look who's talking. You've got a pretty short memory. Remember when I got glasses? You called me four-eyes.★"

"Well, I . . . That's **ancient history**." She **paused**. "Hey, did you say you were coming to my rescue?"

"**Sort of**."

★ **four-eyes** 안경잡이. 안경을 쓴 사람을 낮잡아 이르는 말.

55

"You were, weren't you?" Francine picked up another **plate**. "That was very brave of you, Arthur. Joan of Arc would be **pleased**." She paused. "Want some pizza?"

"Sure."

A little while later, Arthur and Francine **sat back** in their chairs.

"Ohhhh!" Arthur **groan**ed.

"Double ohhhh!" said Francine.

The pizza was gone, and several empty **package**s of **chip**s and cookies were **scatter**ed around.

Arthur smiled. "This is **turn**ing **out** better than I **expect**ed. No **chore**s, no homework, no . . . D.W.!"

He sat up in horror. His sister D.W. had suddenly **appear**ed in the **doorway**.

"Hello, Arthur," she said. "You're in *big* trouble."

Just then, Arthur's father and Francine's mother came around the corner. Ms. Turner

was with them.

"Arthur! Francine!" said Mr. Read.

"**Thank goodness** you're all right!" said Mrs. Frensky.

Ms. Turner shook her head. "I don't know how this could have happened. But I'm glad to see both of you children."

"Are you all right?" asked Mr. Read.

"Are you hurt?" asked Mrs. Frensky.

D.W. took a look around at the chips, the cookies, and the empty pizza box.

"Don't worry," she said. "I think they'll **survive**."

Chapter

10

Monday morning at school, everyone was **crowd**ing around to hear the full story.

"I've always thought," said Binky, "that the characters in books come out to play after the library closes. I don't **suppose** you saw any."

"Of course not," said Francine. "They're **afraid** of the ghosts."

"Ghosts!" said Buster. He **shiver**ed a little.

Francine **nod**ded. "But they didn't **bother** us."

"**Except** for that one with no head," said Arthur. "Right, Francine?"

They **wink**ed at each other.

As the bell rang, the kids **head**ed for their classrooms.

"So, who'd you do your report on?" Buster asked Arthur.

Arthur **stop**ped **short**. Francine would have **bump**ed into him, but she had stopped short, too.

"Report?"

Arthur and Francine **exchange**d a **panic**ky look. In all the excitement, they had forgotten about Joan of Arc.

That look was still on their faces as Muffy finished her report a little while later. The **blackboard** was lined with Crosswire Motors **chart**s and **graph**s.

"And so," she **conclude**d, "it is no **exaggeration** to say that without Edward M. Crosswire, there would be no Elwood City as we know it."

"Very, um, **illuminating**, Muffy," said Mr. Ratburn. "That brings us to"—he looked down at his notes—"Arthur and Francine."

The two partners **shuffle**d up to the front of the room. They stood before the class and **clear**ed **their throats**.

"Um," said Arthur, "we picked Joan of Arc for our report. But we really didn't get a chance to learn as much as we could . . ."

"Because," Francine said suddenly, "we were too busy learning the true meaning of **heroism**. It isn't just the **stuff** you find in books. It's real life."

Arthur **stare**d at her.

"That's right," Francine **went on**. "When we were **lock**ed in the library, it might have been really **terrible**. Actually, it was terrible at first, because we were fighting and everything. Then Arthur came to **rescue** me because he thought I was in danger."

"**Exact**ly," said Arthur. "And Francine was really brave and **resourceful**, too. She found out where the food was. And saved me some pizza."

The class **cheer**ed.

"That's very good," said Mr. Ratburn. "It looks like your **adventure** taught you something important."

Arthur and Francine **beam**ed at each other.

"So I'll give you until tomorrow to do your **assignment**."

"After all we've been through?" said Francine.

"Oh, yes," said Mr. Ratburn. "It should give your report special meaning."

Later that day, Arthur and Buster were walking home from school.

"I hate to say it," said Buster, "but Francine's not so bad."

Arthur nodded. "She can be a lot of fun. She's a good friend."

At that moment, Francine **whiz**zed by on

her bike. She **rode** right through a **puddle**, **splatter**ing the boys with **mud**dy water.

"Sorrryyy!" she **yell**ed over her shoulder.

Arthur and Buster looked down at their wet shirts.

Arthur **sigh**ed. "But nobody's perfect," he said.